T0356111

ADVANCE PRAISE FOR *MURDER BALLADS*

"Beyond wonderful. Written with grace and respect for the history and cultural relevance of this genre. This book has rocked me powerfully."
—**TANYA DONELLY of Belly**

"Refreshing and nuanced. [Katy Horan's] lush and distinctive artwork brings these stories and their characters to vivid life."
—**LISA PERRIN, author of *The League of Lady Poisoners***

"A meticulously researched work that shimmers with empathy . . . an absolute gem and a must-read."
—**MARISSA NADLER, singer-songwriter**

"*Murder Ballads* proves Katy Horan is a master of telling stories through art and a dedicated student of storytelling through song."
—**VALERIE JUNE HOCKETT, singer-songwriter and author of *Light Beams, Somebody to Love,* and *Maps for the Modern World***

"Through [Katy Horan's] sensitive portrayals, the murdered women in these songs—drowned in the rivers of this violent and fascinating history—are paid homage and given proper burial."
—**TAISIA KITAISKAIA, author of *Literary Witches, Ask Baba Yaga,* and *The Nightgown***

"*Murder Ballads* slices through layers of history and interpretation to expose the bits of factual truth behind these grimly beautiful songs . . . deftly describing what has made them endure."
—**WILL SHEFF of Okkervil River**

MURDER BALLADS

Also by Katy Horan

Literary Witches: A Celebration of Magical Women Writers (Illustrator)

The Literary Witches Oracle (Illustrator)

Murder Ballads

ILLUSTRATED LYRICS & LORE

KATY HORAN

Andrews McMeel
PUBLISHING®

Murder Ballads: Illustrated Lyrics & Lore copyright © 2025 by Katy Horan. All rights reserved. Printed in China. No part of this book may be used or reproduced in any manner whatsoever without written permission except in the case of reprints in the context of reviews.

Andrews McMeel Publishing
a division of Andrews McMeel Universal
1130 Walnut Street, Kansas City, Missouri 64106

www.andrewsmcmeel.com

25 26 27 28 29 SDB 10 9 8 7 6 5 4 3 2 1

ISBN: 978-1-5248-8926-5

Library of Congress Control Number: 2024948419

"Delia's Gone" reproduced with permission from Joshua Hampton, *The Silver Dagger: American Murder Ballads* (2020).

"Oh the Wind and Rain" reproduced with permission from Jody Stecher, *Going Up on the Mountain: The Classic First Recordings* (2000).

"Alice Mitchell and Freddy Ward" courtesy of the John Quincy Wolf Folklore Collection at Lyon College in Batesville, Arkansas.

Editor: Melissa Rhodes Zahorsky
Art Director: Diane Marsh
Designer: Brittany Lee
Production Editor: Brianna Westervelt
Production Manager: Julie Skalla

ATTENTION: SCHOOLS AND BUSINESSES
Andrews McMeel books are available at quantity discounts with bulk purchase for educational, business, or sales promotional use. For information, please e-mail the Andrews McMeel Publishing Special Sales Department: sales@andrewsmcmeel.com.

For Daniel, because of course.

He's gonna shoot me down, put my body in the river
Cover me up with the leaves of September
Like an old sad song, you heard it all before
Well, Delia's gone, but I'm settling the score

—Hurray for the Riff Raff, "The Body Electric"

FOREWORD

Around the time I started this piece, Irish film director Paul Duane sent me a link to watch his latest film, *All You Need Is Death.* The premise—especially in the context of this book—was tantalizing: A couple who collects old folk songs discovers a mysterious song that has never been recorded, sung in a now-lost language. They convince a reluctant local to bring them to the only woman who knows the song, passed down to her by generations of women in her family. In the movie, the tune can cause death, and it serves as a reminder of how seditious music can be. The power of a song is also contained within its ability to endure, moving through generations before songs were written down or recorded. Their permanence is rooted in their evolution: take a tune that's easily remembered, swap out the name of a protagonist or political case, and a story can live forever.

Despite their dastardly narratives and terrible outcomes, I've known what murder ballads are since I was a child, even if I didn't know they were called that. They were taught in school, often in Irish, and we sang them as though to be marched to: verse following every terrifying verse, building to an inevitable grisly crescendo. I did not understand why a mother would put a penknife through her own baby's heart, or why scores of women—and it is mostly women—were drowned, battered, or murdered by men. This was also the age when there were hushed warnings about strangers or men in cars who might lure you away, but the world of these songs seemed thrilling and dangerous, as stories often are when they're not happening to you.

When Nick Cave and the Bad Seeds released *Murder Ballads* in 1996, the video for the lead track, "Where the Wild Roses Grow," featured Kylie Minogue bludgeoned to death with a rock, floating Ophelia-like among the reeds. Many murder ballads portray a beautiful post-death stillness instead of the monstrosity of the actual crime. They are songs of revenge against adulterous lovers and spurned advances, of infanticide and jealousy. Many are rooted in misogyny and patriarchy aimed at controlling women who have stepped out of line. Transgressive behavior (premarital sex, getting pregnant outside of marriage, having multiple lovers) could get a gal thrown in a river with her head caved in. But women are not immune to the urge to kill, as recorded in several ballads. A wife in love with another man wants to kill her husband by feeding him "eggs and marrowbone"—it doesn't work out, and she ends up dead. Elsewhere, doomed women turn the tables on men in songs like "The Outlandish Knight" (variations of this include "Pretty Polly" and Irish singer Lisa O'Neill's version, "Along the North Strand").

In Ireland, there is an added darkness to these songs in the context of sociocultural history. Pregnancy outside of marriage led to girls being sent to Magdalene laundries and mother and baby homes. Some took drastic action when faced with crisis, like in "The Cruel Mother" (also known in Ireland as "Weela Weela Walya"), a song sung in Irish playgrounds despite the fact that it's about infanticide. Irish band ØXN (featuring Radie Peat of Lankum) included a version on their 2023 album *CYRM*. Much of their repertoire features songs of women who have been wronged or judged, as a means of redeeming them.

This overlaps with Katy Horan's motivations in this book: to re-examine old narratives, explore who benefits from violence, and acknowledge which voices have been omitted and historically minimized (women, people of color, the poor).

There is something distinctly gothic about the murder ballad, just as there is in all of Katy Horan's drawings. I first encountered her work via The Literary Witches Oracle deck, which featured illustrations of writers alongside objects associated with divination and witchcraft. Her work is rooted in horror, folklore, and mythology, and Horan finds a way to turn familiar tropes into acts of reclamation.

Being an admirer of songs that have origins in violence, patriarchal dominance, and racism (analogous to rap and hip hop, which I have also loved since my teens) is complex. Many of these songs are cautionary tales, usually warning women about propriety and their behavior—and yet they are moving and lush and atmospheric. Immersed in them, we can find ourselves, as Horan writes, "in [a] strange and contradictory place." With her striking visual interpretations, Horan offers a glimpse into the individual lives of the victims, beyond the "dead girl" trope that historically united them all. Her vision of these characters offers a new sense of agency and, as Horan puts it, "a safe space in which to grieve for the women in the rivers."

—**Sinéad Gleeson**

INTRODUCTION

Murder ballads entered my life and imagination in the summer of 2008, in a bar on the Lower East Side of Manhattan. I was in my mid-twenties, living in Brooklyn, teaching after-school art and showing work in small galleries while trying to make it as a freelance illustrator. One night, I went with my boyfriend to see his friend's bluegrass band perform. The bar on Delancey Street was small, dark, and draped in red velvet. The handful of patrons held quiet conversations as they drank and watched the band. Caught up in my own quiet conversation, I didn't pay much attention to the music until the last song began to play. It was a somber tune about a woman drowned by her jealous sister. "Like a golden swan," her body floats downriver, eventually meeting a man who makes a fiddle of her bones and hair. When played, the instrument sings of her murder.

Five years had passed since I'd graduated from art school, and in that time, I'd been drawing and painting witches gathered in the deep woods, horned women knitting sweaters for trees, washerwomen telling their sad tales, and many other scenes rooted in contradiction: beauty and darkness, mystery and familiarity, folksy warmth and unsettling strangeness. In the music of that bone-hair fiddle, I heard an invitation.

That night, I searched for the name of the tune and found it: "Wind and Rain," a version of a much older ballad called "The Twa Sisters." But I couldn't stop there. In the nights, weeks, and months to come, I kept searching, kept reading and listening until I found myself properly entangled in a complex web of songs and their variants. The imagery of the ballads—their flower-laden corpses and bleeding doves—both repelled and entranced me. I wanted to illustrate every single one.

It would be another ten years before I sat down to do so in the form of this book. I can now say that researching, writing about, and illustrating these ballads has deepened our exchange. While my aesthetic appreciation of the genre persists, I see more clearly its roots in patriarchal and white supremacist oppression. In fact, it is in part that tension—between my artistic attraction to murder ballads and my recognition of the problems they contain—that has sustained the creation of this book.

The twenty ballads contained here are those whose imagery I couldn't resist as an artist. At the same time, I tried to keep diversity in mind, wanting to visit the ballads of both Black America and Renaissance Europe, and songs based in myth as well as tales of real murders. I also sought out a range of narratives—although, as you will find, female victims are in the majority. My research was not as conclusive as I would have liked, but I could continue it for another ten years and claim the same. The long histories of these songs, their variations carved like canyons by the continual erosion of time and oral transfer, and the fluid nature of the attending scholarship have made it difficult to feel confident in my grasp of the genre. But its mystery is part of what drew me to these songs in the first place, and what has made them so satisfying (and frustrating) to research.

In my work, I tend toward the shapeshifters—subjects that compel me to render them while also refusing to be pinned down. Yet even for me, studying oral tradition has been a lesson in letting go—in accepting my own limitations, or perhaps the boundaries my subject asserts. Murder ballads almost always chronicle a transgression, a trust betrayed. If I've gained the trust of these songs to any degree, I hope I have honored it in these pages.

I also hope my criticism of the ballads' more challenging aspects isn't mistaken for contempt. Despite their dark legacy, these songs contain an undeniable magic, and under their spell I have found a safe space in which to grieve for the women in the rivers. I hope readers will join me in that strange and contradictory place, if not to grieve, then to contemplate what this genre has to offer—whether beautiful, horrific, or both—and what it can teach us.

HISTORY

A ballad is a narrative song often preserved through oral tradition. A murder ballad, then, is a narrative song that tells of a killing, real or fictitious. Such songs have been a mainstay influence in folk, blues, country music, and beyond. Johnny Cash, Jimi Hendrix, Bob Dylan, and Tom Waits have all made notable recordings in the genre. The tradition of murder balladry itself, however, is much older than American music, with some of the earliest ballads dating to Renaissance Europe.

While many ballads originated and were preserved orally, others began as broadsides or broadsheets, which were large sheets of paper printed with text and woodcut illustration on one side. Advances in literacy and printing technologies between the sixteenth and nineteenth centuries in Europe saw broadsides sold cheaply on the streets, at fairs, and in marketplaces. Early broadsheets focused mostly on religion and politics, but eventually, they contained everything from joke collections and romance stories to reports of recent crimes. Often sold on-site at courthouses and public executions, broadsheets reporting on murders were sometimes intercepted by traveling musicians, who added melodies to the tales, making them accessible to an even wider audience.

As European settlers arrived in America, they brought these ballads with them. Storytelling through song, however, was not a European import to the so-called "New World." Local Indigenous peoples, like others the world over, had long since established their own narrative song traditions. In the context of modern scholarship, however, the history of American balladry generally begins with those songs brought over by the English, Irish, and Scots-Irish in the eighteenth and nineteenth centuries. While the latter two populations eventually settled throughout the United States, they put down especially sturdy musical roots in the Appalachian and Ozark mountain regions, where old and new murder ballads were commonly sung at social gatherings, in kitchens and on porches, transferring (and evolving) from one generation to the next.

EVOLUTION

The basic nature of oral tradition may seem obvious: a person hears someone sing a song, they like the song and want to sing it themselves, and inevitably, the song changes as it travels from person to person and year to year. Anyone who has played a game of "telephone" can understand this,

and yet, there is a vast world of scholarship devoted to understanding the ways in which ballads and their variants evolve.

Some changes are easy enough to trace: the British "Oxford Girl," for example, becomes "Knoxville Girl" or "Waco Girl" in America—place and personal names are amended to suit a changed landscape. Other evolutions are more mysterious, perhaps the result of mishearing, misremembering, or, as the scholars John DeWitt Niles and Eleanor R. Long-Wilgus argue, the "inherently creative" nature of oral song transmission. "Everyone who hears a song and repeats it," they write, "also recreates it."

A singer's creative impulses may also reveal their biases—conscious or unconscious. Over time and on a larger scale, we can see the impacts of shifting social mores on ballad lyrics. For example, the American musicologist George Malcolm Laws points out that, while many older ballads describe sex "constantly and frankly," the same topics are almost universally avoided in American balladry. As a result, early American lyricists were hard-pressed to describe murders that involved sex, such as the killing of one's pregnant lover or the murder of an allegedly unfaithful partner. Likewise, incidences of incest, common in European balladry, are omitted from American variants, as are supernatural motifs, considered equally taboo.

COLLECTION AND SCHOLARSHIP

Ballad collectors and scholarship have always existed together, and ballad collecting as a practice has endured since at least the late seventeenth century. Early collectors such as Samuel Pepys and William Motherwell made notable contributions, but it was the American scholar and folklorist Francis James Child whose collection defined the genre. Published in ten parts between 1882 and 1898, Child's *English and Scottish Popular Ballads* was so influential that scholars began to reference songs using his classification system. Each ballad was assigned a number, and each variant a letter. For example, "The Twa Sisters" became "Child 10," and its twenty-five variants were labeled 10A through 10Y.

But Child's collection, which drew from manuscripts and broadsides, couldn't account for the huge number of ballads that had never been written down. We owe just as much, if not more, to folklorists who wandered the countryside in both Europe and America, collecting songs from the actual "folk" responsible for folk tradition. Cecil J. Sharp, a British collector of the late nineteenth and early twentieth centuries, collected tunes and texts throughout England as well as the hollers of Appalachia. Likewise, the prominent twentieth-century musicologists John and Alan Lomax sought folk treasure among prison gangs and front porch singers throughout the American South.

Among the Lomaxes' archives are spirituals, work songs, and murder ballads composed and sung by Black Americans. Such songs, however, were more often excluded from ballad scholarship, categorized instead as jazz, blues, or ragtime. Indeed, the contributions of Black musicians were—and still are—not only segregated from those of white musicians but taken less seriously by (largely white) scholars and critics. The same pattern persists to this day, evident in the dismissal of rap and R&B songs as "too violent," unworthy of the mainstream praise and analysis enjoyed by equally explicit rock and country lyrics. All this is to say little of the historical theft and appropriation of Black-authored ballads by white artists (*see* "Delia's Gone," page 30, and "Stagolee," page 84) or the tremendous debt owed Black music by virtually every contemporary American music genre.

LEGACY

Just as some "true crime" media does today, murder ballads chronicling real-life murders often took liberties with the facts, flattening complex human stories for purposes of entertainment, emotional manipulation, or both. Interested in weaving a tale as moving and gripping as possible, the typical ballad left no doubt regarding right and wrong, good and evil; it created a clear villain and elicited strong sympathy for the victim.

This was especially true of a popular subgenre known as "murdered-girl" or "murdered-sweetheart" ballads, which featured young women killed by their lovers. Typically, the victim is pregnant by a man to whom she is not wed. Promising to marry her, the father of her child invites her to meet him somewhere or to join him on a journey. Arriving at the riverbank, or in the secluded willow garden, he reveals his violent intentions. There is the requisite pleading by the woman for her life and that of her unborn child, after which the man kills her—by stabbing, beating, or drowning. Except on the rare occasions when her body is buried in a lonely, unmarked grave, the victim is often discarded in the river—a convenient vehicle for the display of her lovely corpse.

The picturesque dead or incapacitated woman is a well-worn trope that has lived in the collective imagination since *Snow White* and *Sleeping Beauty*—probably longer. It relates to a contemporary phenomenon that writer Alice Bolin calls "The Dead Girl Show." Defined as a piece of narrative media whose story begins with the discovery of a female corpse, "The Dead Girl Show" finds expression everywhere from *Law & Order* to David Lynch's *Twin Peaks*, affirming a still-active fascination with slain women's bodies. In the context of murdered-sweetheart ballads, the victim's physical traits—her stature ("little") and complexion ("fair")—serve to emphasize her innocence and heighten the tragedy of her loss. Portrayed as naive and helpless, she is easily led by a cunning male admirer, tricked into a sin that will ultimately destroy her. In death, however, she is "restored" through a complete loss of agency, at last embodying, as the scholar Christina Ruth Hastie writes, "the Victorian ideals . . . of stillness, wholeness, silence, and perfection."

It should come as no surprise, then, that murdered-sweetheart ballads were often wielded as cautionary tales. Young women were to remain chaste and submissive, asserting no desires of their own, lest they meet the same fate as their less careful peers. Some ballads included explicit language to this effect, as in Vernon Dalhart's 1926 recording of "Pearl Bryan":

Young ladies now take warning
Young men are so unjust
It may be your best lover
But you know not whom to trust

Pearl died away from home and friends
Out in that lonely spot
Take heed! Take heed! Believe it girls;
Don't let this be your lot

This message not only admits (and in the same line, dismisses) the apparently homicidal urges of men, but it places the onus of survival directly on women's shoulders. Like the tongue-in-cheek slogan of a certain popular true-crime podcast—"Stay sexy and don't get murdered!"—this warning illustrates the impossible tightrope women are still expected to walk, balancing pressure to fulfill men's desires against the threat of *tempting* them.

Beginning in the early part of the last century, however, a number of musicians have written murder ballads that reclaim the woman's power by casting her as the aggressor, or by using the ballad itself to comment on the historical misogyny of the genre. Songs such as "I Didn't Know the Gun Was Loaded" by Patsy Montana; "The Box It Came In," recorded by Wanda Jackson; "Goodbye Earl," popularized by The Chicks; Gillian Welch's "Caleb Meyer"; "The Body Electric" by Hurray for the Riff Raff; and Taylor Swift's "no body, no crime" all speak to an empowered female agent who takes the matter of a no-good or violent man into her own hands. Hands that once pled for mercy now hold the smoking gun.

OMIE WISE

As is expected of a murdered sweetheart, Naomi "Omie" Wise was indeed very fair. Local clergyman Braxton Craven wrote of her "handsome" face, "her eyes keen yet mild, her words soft and winning." Despite the legendary quality of Craven's description, Naomi was, in fact, a real woman—born in the late 1780s, an orphan who lived with and worked for farmers William and Mary Adams in Randolph County, North Carolina. According to Craven's account, Omie was fetching water from the spring near her home when she met a man named Jonathan Lewis. A resident of neighboring Guilford County, Lewis worked as a clerk in Asheboro, where he boarded with his employer during the week. Riding home on a Saturday, he spotted Omie at the spring and stopped to ask her for a drink. She obliged, and he offered to carry her buckets back to the house. Charmed by Lewis's kindness, or perhaps his smile "like sunbeams bursting through a cloud," Naomi fell in love with him then.

The Adamses warned Omie to steer clear of Lewis. He came from a conniving family and was known to be volatile. But the girl was smitten, and she believed that Lewis intended to marry her. When rumors of their engagement reached Lewis's mother, however, she forbade her son from stopping by the Adamses' farm any longer. Naomi was left heartbroken.

At his mother's insistence, Lewis began courting Hettie (sometimes "Hattie") Elliott—the sister of his wealthy employer. And yet the rumors of his engagement to Naomi continued. Hettie confronted Lewis about the story, but he denied it, swearing that he was true.

In April of 1807, Naomi Wise set out once more to the Adamses' spring, but she never returned. A search party later discovered her footprints leading to a tree stump from which hoofprints led away, indicating that she had used the stump to mount a horse. Her body was found tangled in the weeds along the shore of Deep River. Noting bruises on her neck, the coroner ruled her death a "drowning by violence." He also discovered that she had been pregnant.

Lewis was immediately suspected of the murder. Though captured and jailed, he escaped thirty days later and fled the region. Several years passed before he was found and brought back to North Carolina, where he finally faced trial. But by that time, many witnesses had either died or left the area, and Lewis was acquitted due to a lack of evidence. On his deathbed, however, Lewis is said to have confessed, revealing that Naomi's ghost had been torturing him for years.

We don't know what Lewis said to get Omie to mount his horse that fateful day, but most accounts suggest that he had asked her to meet him at the spring, promising to whisk her away and marry her. If this is true, it aligns eerily well with a hallmark of the fictional ballads in this genre, in which the killer invites his supposed lover to join him on a journey of some kind—for "some pleasures to see" (as in "Pretty Polly") or "to take an evenin's walk" (as in "Knoxville Girl"). Indeed, many aspects of Naomi's story fit neatly into the murdered-sweetheart mold, raising questions about whether Craven's telling—and the ballads it influenced—stretched the facts.

Contemporary scholarship reveals that Naomi may not have been the picture of maidenly naivety Craven suggests. In her book on the topic, folklorist Eleanor Long-Wilgus cites an earlier poem by Mary Woody—an alleged witness to the crime, or perhaps its immediate aftermath—which offers a different portrait of Naomi. Based on that portrait, Long-Wilgus theorizes that Naomi was in fact older than Lewis, "carrying on with him" despite knowing he was engaged to another woman. At the time of their affair (and the resulting pregnancy), according to Woody's account, Naomi was already the mother of two children born out of wedlock. In North Carolina, "illegitimate" children were denied any inheritance from the father, so "bastardy bonds," similar to modern child-support payments, were levied instead. Long-Wilgus suggests that Lewis, who was not a wealthy man, offered to pay Naomi in exchange for not naming him the father. She argues that Naomi met with Lewis not because she believed in false promises of marriage and "fine things" but because she'd been offered a sensible deal.

The Naomi presented in Woody's poem has agency and awareness—qualities that both distance her from the murdered-sweetheart archetype and reveal her deeper humanity. But ballads are not judged by their historical accuracy, nor are the women who actually *lived* the ones the lyrics often mourn. As remembered in song, Naomi Wise is the perfect victim: simple, guileless, pure. Craven's account sought to maximize the tragedy of her death, and like many ballad authors of the time, he did so by rendering her in two dimensions—a surface on which to project a fantasy.

A seminal version of the Naomi Wise ballad is credited to the fiddle player G. B. Grayson. A recording of his rendition was released in 1928. Grayson's "Ommie Wise" contains several hallmarks of the murdered-sweetheart genre: the victim's blind trust, the villain's promise of a journey, the reveal of his true intentions, and the victim's pleas to spare her life. The ending, however, is unusually true to the facts, admitting that Lewis escaped punishment (in this version, to join the army) rather than face the gallows with remorse, as most sweetheart-killers did.

Other notable early to mid-twentieth-century variants include Shirley Collins's 1959 "Omie Wise" and Doc Watson's 1964 "Little Omie Wise." Many contemporary musicians and bands have added to the Naomi Wise corpus, including Elvis Costello, Bob Dylan, and Okkervil River.

"Ommie Wise"

G. B. Grayson, 1927 record single

I'll tell you all a story about Ommie Wise
How she was deluded by John Lewis's lies

He told her to meet him at Adams's spring
He'd bring her some money and some other fine things
He brought her no money nor no other fine things
But "Get up behind me, Ommie, to Squire Ellett's we'll go"

She got up behind him, "So carefully we'll go"
They rode 'til they came where deep waters did flow
John Lewis, he concluded to tell her his mind
John Lewis, he concluded to leave her behind

She threw her arms around him; "John, spare me my life
And I'll go distracted and never be your wife"

He threw her arms from 'round him, and into the water she plunged
John Lewis, he turned 'round and rode back to Adams's hall
He went inquiring for Ommie, but "Ommie, she is not here
She's gone to some neighbor's house and won't be gone very long"

John Lewis was took a prisoner and locked up in the jail
Was locked up in the jail around, was there to remain a while
John Lewis, he stayed there for six months or maybe more
Until he broke jail; into the army he did go

THE CRUEL MOTHER

Pregnant by her father's clerk following a secret affair, a woman goes into labor, giving birth to twins (or, in some variants, a single baby, or triplets). Recognizing the difficulties of caring for children as an unwed mother, or perhaps overcome with shame at giving birth out of wedlock, she stabs her infants in the heart with a penknife and buries them in the cold ground. Later, she encounters a group of children "playing at ball" and, in her grief, tells them how lovingly she would treat them "if you were mine." Two of the children reveal they are the ghosts of the twins she just bore and murdered and let her know, in no uncertain terms, that she is condemned to hell.

This is a common narrative version of "The Cruel Mother," the origins of which can be traced to a seventeenth-century British broadside titled "The Duke's Daughter's Cruelty." Part of the revenant subgenre of ballads in which victims return as ghosts, often to issue warnings or inflict shame, "The Cruel Mother" was interpreted as a cautionary tale for women about the dangers of straying from accepted sexual mores. At this time in history, infanticide was not uncommon. Unwed mothers faced risks to their health and immense social, economic, and even legal repercussions. In 1609 in England, a statute was passed that mandated a prison term of one year for mothers whose "illegitimate" children were supported by government welfare. Even if she avoided incarceration, an unwed mother faced a life of extreme poverty and physical danger—for both herself and her children. Add shame to the mix, and one can easily imagine the pressure on women to conceal out-of-wedlock pregnancies, one way or another. But infanticide was even more reviled than the unwed mothers were themselves, and ballads like "The Duke's Daughter's Cruelty" flourished within the socially conservative broadside market, spawning "The Cruel Mother" and many more variants.

Ironically, it is the mother's anguish—not her cruelty—that has endeared the ballad to listeners across the centuries. The song's narrative circumstances, particularly the mother's pain and sorrow, remain familiar, to some degree, to many women. The iconic folk singers Shirley Collins and Joan Baez are among the slew of female musicians to have recorded versions of the ballad. In the liner notes to her 1959 album, *False True Lovers,* Collins is quoted summing up the song's modern legacy: "While I feel very sorry for the murdered babes, my deep sympathy lies with the poor mother."

H. E. D. Hammond collected a variant of the ballad from a Mrs. Case of Cerne Abbas, Dorset, England, and printed part of it in the *Journal of the Folk-Song Society* in 1907. These lyrics follow the song's traditional narrative, though they omit any mention of the woman's courtship by her father's clerk, beginning instead with the twins' birth. Unlike the ghost children in other variants, those described by Mrs. Case don't explicitly condemn their mother to hell, but remind her, scornfully, of her deeds. Some variants, such as the Irish "Weela Weela Walya," list the earthly consequences the mother will endure (namely, jailtime and execution), while others go on to describe a succession of post-death torments, each of which will last seven years: "Seven years a fish in the flood," "seven years a tongue in the warning bell," and "seven years a bird in the wood" are all common and are generally followed by "seven years in the flames of hell."

"The Cruel Mother"

Collected by H. E. D. Hammond from Mrs. Case of Cerne Abbas, Dorset, England,
for the *Journal of the Folk-Song Society,* Vol. 3, No. 11

She laid herself back against a thorn,
All aloney, aloney,
And there she had two pretty babes born,
Down by the greenwood sidey.

She had a penknife long and sharp,
All aloney, aloney,
And she pressed it through their tender hearts
Down by the greenwood sidey.

She digged a grave both wide and deep,
All aloney, aloney,
And she buried them under the marble stone.
Down by the greenwood sidey.

As she was set in her Father's hall,
All aloney, aloney,
Oh! there she saw two pretty babes playing at ball,
Down by the greenwood sidey.

"Oh! babes, Oh! babes if you were mine,
All aloney, aloney,
I would dress you up in the scarlet fine,"
Down by the greenwood sidey.

"Oh! Mother, Oh! mother, we once were thine,
All aloney, aloney,
You did not dress us in the scarlet fine.
Down by the greenwood sidey.

You digged a grave both wide and deep,
All aloney, aloney,
And you buried us under the marble stone."
Down by the greenwood sidey.

DELIA'S GONE

In the late 1920s, Robert Winslow Gordon, the founder of the Archive of American Folk Song at the Library of Congress, set out to find the true story behind a ballad called "Delia." Although he succeeded, he did not publish his findings. The true "Delia" remained lost until 2000, when chemistry professor–turned–song collector John Garst, working from what little of Gordon's research survived, uncovered a news report, trial transcripts, and other documents that told the true story of Delia Green: a fourteen-year-old Black girl who was killed in 1900 in Savannah, Georgia.

Delia worked as a maid in the home of Willie and Emma West. The Wests hosted a Christmas Eve party that Delia and her fourteen-year-old boyfriend, Moses Houston, both attended. Although the defense claimed it was a raucous party where everyone was drunk, the Wests testified that it was a quiet, intimate get-together—and that Houston was the only intoxicated guest. He had been paid to retrieve Mr. West's handgun from the repair shop earlier that day and allegedly kept it hidden under a napkin throughout the evening. A fight erupted when a very drunk Houston, perhaps seeking to impress his fellow guests, loudly announced that he had been sleeping with Delia. When Delia protested, he grew more adamant, claiming he had "had [her] as many times as [he had] fingers and toes." Houston then motioned as though to leave but instead grabbed Mr. West's gun, turned, and shot Delia in the groin. Houston tried to flee, but West caught him and turned him over to the police. Houston confessed immediately, saying he would shoot her again if he could. Delia was taken to her mother's home and died the next day.

Houston pleaded not guilty in court despite his earlier confession to the police, and during the trial, he wore more childlike clothing to emphasize his youth. Willie Mills, a witness for the defense, testified that upon returning from the repair shop with the gun, Houston tussled with his friend Eddie Cohen, accidentally firing and striking Delia. Another witness, however, testified that Willie Mills was not present at the time of the shooting, and Eddie Cohen himself asserted he had left the party prior to the incident. During their testimony, the Wests told the court that Houston had murdered Delia without provocation.

Ultimately, the jury declared Houston guilty, but they recommended that the judge exercise mercy on such a young man. The judge complied, sentencing Houston not to death but to life in prison. Houston served twelve and a half years before being paroled in 1913. Little is known of his later life, except that he may have died in New York in 1927, when he was still quite young.

Although Delia's murder made local headlines at the time, it quickly faded from public memory, likely overshadowed by coverage of alleged Black-on-white crime (and the lynchings that often followed), considered more newsworthy than a young Black girl's murder. Instead, Delia's story was left to the mercy of the balladeers, and they did not treat her kindly.

Songs about Delia may share narrative DNA with other ballads about murdered women, but certain differences between Delia's portrait and those of her white counterparts point to undercurrents of American misogynoir—the contempt for and ingrained bias against Black women. Many murder ballads, including "Delia" or "Delia's Gone," are sung from the perspective of the killer, yet even so, their white victims are typically described in terms of their beauty and virtue (which are often intertwined): "that dear little girl," the white victim is called, or "lady fair," known for her "lily white hands" and "golden curls." Delia is afforded much less sympathy—or she is outright maligned, as in Johnny Cash's well-known 1994 rendition of the song. An update to his less hateful, but hardly reverent 1962 version, Cash's later recording is rife with violent fantasies and portrays Delia as a loathsome character who deserved her fate. While Cash's narrator's contempt sits at one end of the spectrum, most other variants range from hostile to unflattering. Many include the refrain "one more rounder gone," a phrase believed to be a reference to Delia herself. In a 1911 article for *Journal of American Folklore*, the sociologist Howard W. Odum writes that a rounder is "a worthless and wandering person," and points out how unusual it was for a woman to be referred to as such. Likewise, Blind Willie McTell's "Little Delia," recorded in 1940, accuses Delia of being "a gambler"—a detail that Bob Dylan also includes in his 1993 version. Pete Seeger's 1954 variant is somewhat kinder, referring to "poor Delia," but it fails to paint a picture of its central figure or express any sorrow over her loss. Perhaps the only "Delia" variant to properly honor or grieve Delia Green is that of the Caribbean American folk and calypso singer Harry Belafonte, who, also in 1954, recorded a version in which he does not sing as Delia's killer but as someone who loved and mourns for her.

Ultimately, the "Delia" tradition has its roots in the Black community. While the original author of the song remains unknown, the earliest "Delia" fragment was published in Odum's article—a selection of folk songs and poems collected from Black people in the American South—under the title "One Mo' Rounder Gone." In 1924, the Black musician and entrepreneur Reese Du Pree expanded on this fragment in a recording for OKeh Records, and about a decade later, folklorists Alan Lomax and Mary Elizabeth Barnicle collected a Bahamian version performed by the Nassau String Band. The song became much more well-known when in 1939 a Black Chicago bandleader named Jimmie Gordon recorded a version titled "Delhia" that featured elements of ragtime, jazz, and blues, inspiring a wide range of variants including those by McTell and Seeger, who in turn inspired white artists such as Pat Boone, Waylon Jennings, and Bob Dylan to contribute renditions.

using selections from primary sources as well as memories from his own family's singing traditions, this version includes several important motifs. The phrase "Delia's gone, one more round, Delia's gone" is nearly universal across the "Delia" tradition, as is mention of the "rubber-tired buggy, double-seated hack" in which Delia's body is taken to the graveyard. While Hampton's lyrics do outline the narrator's violence against Delia, they do not seek to shame her. As in many variants, including both of Johnny Cash's, the narrator of Hampton's song describes the sound of Delia's ghostly footsteps in his cell, which keeps him from sleep, implying perhaps a glimmer of remorse.

Joshua Hampton includes a composite version of "Delia's Gone" in his 2020 book, *The Silver Dagger: American Murder Ballads.* Arranged by Hampton

"Delia's Gone"

Joshua Hampton, *The Silver Dagger: American Murder Ballads*

Delia, oh, Delia, Delia all my life,
If I hadn't shot poor Delia,
She might have become my wife,
Delia's gone, one more round, Delia's gone.

First time I shot her, I shot her in the side,
The second time I shot her,
She bowed her head and died,
Delia's gone, one more round, Delia's gone.

Rubber-tired buggy, double-seated hack,
Takin' poor Delia to the graveyard,
And ain't gonna bring her back,
Delia's gone, one more round, Delia's gone.

Sixty-four years in prison, judge, that ain't
    no time,
I got a brother in New Orleans,
Doing nine hundred ninety and nine,
Delia's gone, one more round, Delia's gone.

Jailer, oh jailer, jailer, I can't sleep,
Because all around my bedside,
I hear the patter of little Delia's feet,
Delia's gone, one more round, Delia's gone.

Now some gave Delia a nickel, others gave
    a dime,
But I didn't give her one doggone cent,
Because that girl was mine,
Delia's gone, one more round, Delia's gone.

IN THE PINES

The ballad known as "In the Pines" developed like a snowball of fragments, with innumerable singers mixing and matching different pieces to create a densely packed but widely variable tradition. The results tend to be narratively vague but consistently atmospheric and haunted, centering on a cold, piney wood in which a woman (or, at times, the singer) "shiver[s] the whole night through." Commonly, the singer refers to the woman as "my girl," implying a romantic relationship between the two. However, in some variants, the singer also describes the woman as having (or having had) a husband. In any case, the woman is often addressed with hostility and suspicion, suggesting she has been unfaithful to her lover and is sleeping in the wood as some sort of punishment or penance. Sometimes, she—or her husband—is decapitated in a horrible accident involving the driving wheel of a train.

Unless you believe in homicidal locomotives, there is no murder in "In the Pines," but the ballad has evolved in ways that lead the imagination to dark and menacing places—places that, to anyone versed in the bloody ways of murder ballads, feel quite familiar.

While collecting folk songs in Appalachia in 1917, British folklorist Cecil Sharp sourced the earliest documented fragment of the song from a Miss Lizzie Abner in Kentucky. Titled "Black Girl," it opens with the warning "Black girl, black girl, don't lie to me." (This becomes "my girl, my girl" in other variants.) The question "Where did you sleep last night?" follows, and is answered: "I stayed in the pines where the sun never shines and shivered when the cold wind blows." Although the song's tone is threatening, it doesn't explicitly culminate in anyone's death. Later variants, however, go on to introduce the detail of the train accident, which seems to have been absorbed from a lesser-known ballad called "The Longest Train." In 1925, Robert Winslow Gordon recorded the first variant to include the beheading-by-train detail, and just a year later, Doctor Coble "Dock" Walsh released a commercial recording of the evolved ballad.

In the 1940s, renditions by bluegrass musician Bill Monroe and blues artist Huddie Ledbetter, better known as "Lead Belly," formed two distinct branches within the ballad's lineage. Monroe's 1941 recording does not mention violence or death of any kind. Perhaps taking after "The Longest Train," it winds through the cold and lonesome pines, but without much sense of danger. By contrast, Lead

Belly's recordings (published under various titles, from "Where Did You Sleep Last Night?" to "Black Girl," beginning in 1944) reinstate the interrogative opening of Sharp's original fragment. In the end, it is the woman's husband who loses his head to a train. While there is no murder exactly, some interpret Lead Belly's accusatory tone, together with the shadowy mood of the song and the addition of the train accident, to indicate the presence of something or someone sinister.

That "something" sinister is certainly present in Nirvana's 1993 performance of "Where Did You Sleep Last Night" for *MTV Unplugged.* Lead singer and guitarist Kurt Cobain introduces the song as written by Lead Belly, which is true in the sense that Cobain's rendition is clearly descended from the blues singer's strain. But unlike Lead Belly's, Cobain's performance is agonized, culminating in abrasive screams that will go on to haunt listeners, considering Cobain's suicide just five months later. "The way he delivered that song," the music journalist Eric Weisbard remarked of the performance, as quoted in an article for *Slate,* "it really felt like he was almost foreseeing his own demise."

That sense of eerie foreboding, expressed to varying degrees, is what characterizes the whole of the "In the Pines" tradition. Whether sung in Monroe's lilting, lonesome tenor, Lead Belly's powerful bass, or Cobain's tortured howl, the ballad possesses a certain unnameable darkness that may ultimately derive from its *lack* of a violent climax.

Dock Walsh recorded the ballad's commercial debut in 1926. Among the first known variants to combine the lyrics "in the pines" and "the longest train" together with mention of the train accident, Walsh's version evidences the song's patchwork history. In it, however, the singer does not demand to know where his "girl" slept; in fact, *he* is the one who "shivered when the cold wind blow."

"In the Pines"

"Dock" Walsh, 1926 record single

In the pines, in the pines, where the sun never shine,
And I shivered when the cold wind blow.

Oh, if I'd minded what Grandma said,
Oh, where would I been tonight?

I'd-a been in the pines, where the sun never shine,
And shivered when the cold wind blow.

The longest train I ever saw
Went down the Georgia line.

The engine is stopped at a six-mile post,
The cabin never left the town.

Now darling, now darling, don't tell me no lie,
Where did you stay last night?

I stayed in the pines, where the sun never shine,
And I shivered when the cold wind blow.

The prettiest little girl that I ever saw
Went walking down the line.

Her hair it was of a curly type,
Her cheeks was rosy red.

Now darling, now darling, don't tell me no lie,
Where did you stay last night?

I stayed in the pines, where the sun never shine,
And I shivered when the cold wind blow.

The train run back one mile from town
And killed my girl, you know.

Her head was caught in the driver wheel,
Her body I never could find.

Oh darling, oh darling, don't tell me no lie,
Where did you stay last night?

I stayed in the pines, where the sun never shine,
And I shivered when the cold wind blow.

The best of friends is to part sometimes,
And why not you and I?

Now darling, oh darling, don't tell me no lie,
Where did you stay last night?

I stayed in the pines, where the sun never shine,
And I shivered when the cold wind blow.

Oh, transportation has brought me here,
Take a money for to carry me away.

Oh darling, now darling, don't tell me no lie,
Where did you stay last night?

I stayed in the pines, where the sun never shine,
And I shivered when the cold wind blow.

THE BLOODY GARDENER

A man of noble birth falls in love with a shepherd's daughter. His disapproving mother sends a letter to the woman, pretending to be her son and asking the woman to meet him in the garden. When the woman arrives, expecting to find her true love waiting, she is instead met by a "bloody gardener." He accuses her of attempting to steal his beautiful flowers, then either cuts her throat or stabs her to death before burying her beneath a flower bed "in the way her virtuous body never should be found." The son arrives in the garden, believing he is to meet his love. He searches until he sees a snow-white dove perch above him in a myrtle tree. The bird's breast begins to bleed, revealing (in a way unique to folklore and balladry) the fate of his beloved. He runs home to confront his mother, vowing to "take flight" with his darling—that is, to take his own life.

A core theme of "The Bloody Gardener" is one commonly found in murder ballads: parental opposition to a son's love for a woman of perceived lower class—in this case, the shepherd's daughter. This is made plain in the original broadside, titled "The Bloody Gardener's Cruelty; or, The Shepherd's Daughter Betray'd," printed in London in 1754:

His parents they were all of high degree,
They said, She is no match at all for thee.
If you our blessing have, grant us but what
*   we crave,*
And wed with none but whom we shall
*   agree.*

While the twenty-seven-stanza broadside and a similar version included in a 1769 Scottish pamphlet are both well-preserved, the ballad has received relatively little attention from scholars. In 1929, however, English folklorist Maud Karpeles collected a version from a Mrs. May McCabe of North River, Conception Bay, Newfoundland. In 1965, musician Kenneth Peacock published a fourteen-stanza version entitled "The Bloody Garden" in his *Songs of the Newfoundland Outports, Vol. 3.*

Popular during the broadside days, the song was also a favorite of musicians during Britain's mid-twentieth-century folk revival. Albert Lancaster "A. L." Lloyd, a major figure of the movement, theorized that the song held such sway over the centuries due to "the contrast between the gardener's gentle profession and his murderous nature." Perhaps for this reason, Lloyd, Martin Carthy, and many other prominent British folk revivalists all produced well-loved recordings.

The Newfoundland variant collected by Maud Karpeles in 1929 is interesting in that it preserves the supernatural elements present in the original broadside. While many British ballads that crossed the Atlantic did so at the cost of their talking animals and magical objects, "The Bloody Gardener" retained its "milk-white dove" who, by drooping her wings and "[bleeding] fresh," effectively tattles on the murderer. And though the murderer in this story is not the victim's lover, the song also contains some elements common to murdered-sweetheart ballads, including the lyric "he took out his knife, cut the single thread of life," which appears in various forms across the tradition.

"The Bloody Gardener"

Sung in 1929 by Mrs. May McCabe of North River, Conception Bay, Newfoundland.
Collected by Maud Karpeles in *Folk Songs from Newfoundland*.

'Twas of a lady fair, a shepherd's daughter dear,
She was courted by her own sweetheart's delight,
But false letters mother wrote: Meet me dear my heart's delight
For it's about some business I have to relate.

O this young maid arose and to the garden goes
In hopes to meet her own true heart's delight.
She searched the ground and no true love she found,
Till at length a bloody gardener appeared in view.

He says: My lady gay, what brought you here this way,
Or have you come to rob me of my garden gay?
She cries: No thief I am, I'm in search of a young man,
Who promised that he'd meet me here this way.

Prepare, prepare, he cried, prepare to lose your life.
I'll lay your virtuous body to bleed in the ground,
And with flowers fine and gay your grave I'll overlay
In the way your virtuous body never will be found.

He took out his knife, cut the single thread of life,
And he laid her virtuous body to bleed in the ground,
And with flowers fine and gay her grave he overlaid
In the way her virtuous body never should be found.

This young man arose and into the garden goes
In hopes to meet his own true heart's delight.
He searched the garden round, but no true love he found
Till the groves and the valleys seemed with him to mourn.

44

O he sat down to rest on a mossy bank so sweet
Till a milk-white dove come perching round his face,
And with battering wings so sweet all around this young man's feet,
But when he arose this dove she flew away.

The dove she flew away and perched on a myrtle tree
And the young man called after her with speed.
This young man called after her with his heart filled with woe,
Until he came to where the dove she lay.

He said: My pretty dove, what makes you look so sad,
Or have you lost your love as I have mine?
When down from a tree so tall, down on her grave did fall,
She drooped her wings and shook her head and bled fresh from the breast.

O this young man arose and unto his home did go,
Saying: Mother dear, you have me undone;
You have robbed me of my dear, my joy and my delight,
So it's alone with my darling I'll soon take flight.

THE TWA SISTERS

It's a story both ancient and familiar: Two sisters love the same man, but he chooses the "fairer" and/or younger one. In this ballad, the sisters go walking by a river, and, filled with murderous jealousy, the less fair and/or elder sister pushes the other into the water to drown. The drowned sister's body eventually floats ashore at a miller's dam, where a passing fiddler uses her bones and hair to construct a magic fiddle that, when played, reveals the truth of the murder.

This ballad's spotty history begins with a seventeenth-century broadside printed in London titled "The Miller and the King's Daughter," but folklorists disagree about whether the song is British in origin. Early versions also appear in Norway, Iceland, the Faroe Islands, Sweden, and mainland Denmark, suggesting possible Scandinavian ancestry, but the lineage isn't clear—and it grows even more complex as the song travels throughout Britain and on to America.

Scholars often marvel at the immense diversity among variants of "The Twa Sisters." Indeed, a number of core narrative variations have been noted, primarily the inclusion or exclusion of the bone-hair fiddle (or harp, in some cases). The magical instrument can be found in English, Scottish, and American versions of the ballad, but many variants (from all three countries, especially the US) omit the singing fiddle altogether. In its place, there are a few alternate endings, including one where the attacked sister survives in the river until she comes to the miller's pond. The miller rescues her, only to rob her of her jewels and finery before pushing her back into the water, where she finally drowns. Others include the discovery and subsequent burial of the drowned sister and a variety of punishments for the jealous sister and thieving miller.

The most prominent narrative strain contains ballads in which the singing fiddle plays a large part, as does a haunting refrain: "Oh, the wind and rain." Among these, Gillian Welch's version for the soundtrack to the 2000 film *Songcatcher* titled "Wind and Rain" is likely the best known today. The refrain traces its origins, however, to at least 1937, when ballad collector Phillips Barry published a Virginian variant containing the "wind and rain" phrase. Thirty years later, writer George Foss obtained two very similar versions along the Virginia–North Carolina border. One of these was performed by Dan Tate, who called it "Wind and Rain," and from there, it was embraced without much deviation by countless American and English folk revivalists.

Though I didn't know its title at the time, it was a live performance of "Wind and Rain" that introduced me to the world of murder ballads. While I sat in a bar in New York in 2008, this song beckoned me into the overgrown garden, whispered to me from the gate, promising beauty, horror, sorrow, and most importantly, an enchanted fiddle made of human remains.

"Oh the Wind and Rain," by American revival singer Jonathan "Jody" Stecher, was not the first ballad to make use of the "wind and rain" refrain, but it's the version that clearly inspired later recordings by Jerry Garcia, Gillian Welch, and many other folk and bluegrass musicians. Stecher's iconic recording first appeared on his 1977 album, *Going Up on the Mountain.* A modified version was later included on *Oh the Wind and Rain: Eleven Ballads*, released in 1999, and the original recording was again released on Stecher's 2000 reissue, *Going Up on the Mountain: The Classic First Recordings,* which combines material from the 1977 album and one other from that decade.

"Oh the Wind and Rain"

Jody Stecher, *Going Up on the Mountain: The Classic First Recordings*

Now, there were two sisters come a-walking down the stream
Oh, the wind and rain
One came behind, pushed the other one in
Crying, oh, the dreadful wind and rain

Johnny gave the youngest one a gay gold ring
Oh, the wind and rain
Didn't give the oldest one anything
Crying, oh, the dreadful wind and rain

She pushed her in the river to drown
Oh, the wind and rain
And watched her as she floated down
Crying, oh, the dreadful wind and rain

She floated 'til she came to the miller's pond
Oh, the wind and rain
Crying, "Father, oh father, there swims a swan"
Crying, oh, the dreadful wind and rain

And the miller fished her out with his drifting hook
Oh, the wind and rain
And he brought this maiden from the brook
Crying, oh, the dreadful wind and rain

He laid her on the bank to dry
Oh, the wind and rain
And a fiddling fool came passing by
Crying, oh, the dreadful wind and rain

Down the road come a fiddler fair
Oh, the wind and rain
Away down the road come a fiddler fair
Crying, oh, the dreadful wind and rain

Down the road come a fiddler fair
Oh, the wind and rain
He took thirty strands of her long yellow hair
Crying, oh, the dreadful wind and rain

He made a fiddle bow of her long yellow hair
Oh, the wind and rain
Made a fiddle bow of her long yellow hair
Crying, oh, the dreadful wind and rain

And he made fiddle pegs of her long finger bones
Oh, the wind and rain
He made fiddle pegs of her long finger bones
Crying, oh, the dreadful wind and rain

And he made a little fiddle of her breastbone
Oh, the wind and rain
Whose sound would melt a heart of stone
Crying, oh, the dreadful wind and rain

And the only tune that the fiddle would play
Was "Oh, the wind and rain"
The only tune that the fiddle would play
Was "Oh, the dreadful wind and rain"

LIZIE WAN

A young woman called Lizie Wan (or Lucy Wan, Rosie Ann, or Fair Lucy) confesses to her father that she is pregnant with her brother's child. The brother, enraged by her betrayal, beheads Lizie with his "good broad sword" and cuts her body into three pieces. He then rushes to his mother, who questions him about his bloodied weapon. He lies at first, claiming he used it to kill his disobedient greyhound. Unconvinced, the mother presses him again, and he admits to his crime. The mother asks what her son will do "when thy father comes h[o]me," to which the son replies that he will drown himself in the sea.

This tragic ballad first appears in the anthologist David Herd's *Ancient and Modern Scottish Songs, Heroic Ballads, Etc.*, a manuscript dating to 1776. Because of this, there is not much debate over Lizie's Scottish origins, but the ballad also has a lengthy history in America, the earliest record of which may be the expanded adaptation "The Bloody Brother," published in *The Forget Me Not Songster,* a collection of ballads printed in New York in 1840. Francis Child also includes two variants of "Lizie Wan" in his collection: one sourced from the Herd manuscript and the other, titled "Rosie Ann," from the collection of the Scottish poet William Motherwell. Cecil Sharp later identified a variant titled "Lizzie Wan" in Kentucky in 1917.

Although "Lizie Wan" is a more stable ballad than many, her import to America resulted in certain changes—perhaps to suit the tastes of a new audience. American folklorist Tristram P. Coffin outlines a version of the ballad found in early twentieth-century America in which Lizie confesses to being pregnant but does not name her brother as the father. The brother does, however, kill her—for reasons that are unclear in this version. While a brother's killing of his unwed pregnant sister isn't difficult to imagine in the context of murder balladry, it is likely that the change resulted from an effort to censor the theme of incest. Nevertheless, the original storyline has persisted over the years, preserved in both British and (some) American variants. In fact, Kate Bush's 1978 song "The Kick Inside" was apparently inspired by "Lizie Wan." On a promotional cassette, Bush explains that, with "The Kick Inside," she intended to explore "an area . . . that is really untouched"—that of incest. "There are so many songs about love," she says, "but they are always on such an obvious level."

Cecil Sharp collected "Lizzie Wan" from Mr. Ben J. Finlay in Manchester, Clay County, Kentucky, on August 10, 1917. Interestingly, this version excludes any description of the murder itself, wherein (per Herd's manuscript) the brother "cutted off Lizie Wan's head, and hir fair body in three." It also modifies the son's fate. In the Finlay variant, when the mother asks what her son will do, he says he will board "some little ship" and "sail plumb over the sea," but in the Herd ballad, he says he will "set his foot into a bottomless boat, and swim to the sea ground"—implying he will drown himself.

"Lizzie Wan"

Sung in 1917 by Mr. Ben J. Finlay of Manchester, Clay County, Kentucky.

Collected by Cecil Sharp in *English Folk Songs from the Southern Appalachians*, vol. 1.

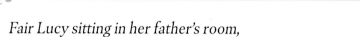

Fair Lucy sitting in her father's room,
Lamenting and a-making her mourn;
And in steps her brother James:
O what's fair Lucy done?

It is time for you to weep,
Lamenting and a-making your mourn.
Here's a babe at my right side,
And it is both mine and yourn.

O what will you do when your father comes home?
Dear son, come tell to me.
I'll set my foot into some little ship
And I'll sail plumb over the sea.

O what will you do with your house and land?
Dear son, come tell to me.
I'll leave it here, my old, dear mother;
Be kind to my children three.

O what will you do with your pretty little wife?
Dear son, come tell to me.
She can set her foot in another little ship
And follow after me.

Back home, back home will you return?
Dear son, come tell to me.
When the sun and moon sets in yon hill,
And I hope that'll never be.

PEARL BRYAN

Without knowing the specific circumstances of Pearl Bryan's horrible death, one might regard her ballad as another pregnant-woman-murdered-for-being-pregnant song (common within the murdered-sweetheart subgenre). But Pearl's pregnancy played a much more loaded role in her demise: she was seeking an abortion, and she was killed by the very people who'd said they would help her.

On the first day of February, 1896, in the Kentucky town of Fort Thomas just across the river from Cincinnati, Ohio, an orchard worker by the name of John Hewling came across a young woman's body on his employer's land. Her clothes were in disarray, her skirt pulled up over her shoulders. It wasn't until the sheriff and coroner arrived on the scene, however, that the more gruesome discovery was made: her head was missing. What's more, the coroner's examination revealed the decapitated woman had been four to five months pregnant.

Armed with these details, the local papers feasted on the story, and it wasn't long before the Bryans of Greencastle, Indiana, caught wind of it. Although the victim had not yet been named, the family worried she might be their Pearl, who had left home for Indianapolis a few days prior. Sadly, the Bryans were right to worry; it turned out that the victim wore unusually petite shoes made by a small Ohio company, and detectives were able to trace them to the shop in Greencastle where twenty-three-year-old Pearl Bryan was one of three customers who wore that size. The other two women were found to be alive and well, leaving little doubt as to the victim's identity. The next day, two young men were arrested and charged with the murder: Scott Jackson and his roommate, Alonzo Walling.

Jackson and Walling claimed that William Wood, their friend and Pearl's second cousin, had gotten Pearl pregnant and had sent her to them for an abortion. They were both dental students, so they had some medical knowledge and training, but—they said—they'd given her too much cocaine (a common anesthetic at the time), and she'd died of an overdose. The men admitted to removing Pearl's head to prevent identification. Meanwhile, A. W. Early, a friend of William Wood and the manager of the Western Union telegraph office in Greencastle, claimed to have seen letters exchanged between Wood and Jackson in which Jackson "admitted his intimacy with Pearl, and his responsibility for her present condition." Jackson had furnished "recipes calculated to prevent the evil results of their indiscretion" and had urged Wood to give them to Pearl. Wood did so, but Pearl remained pregnant, at which point Jackson suggested that she come to Cincinnati, where he would arrange for her to have an abortion. It is almost certain, then, that Jackson was both the father of Pearl's baby and her killer. The autopsy revealed that Pearl had died not of a cocaine overdose but of a lethal injection of prussic acid. Although it's unclear whether the substance was intended to kill Pearl or induce a miscarriage, Jackson and Walling's earlier lies paint a dark picture. Later that spring and summer, they were tried and convicted, then hanged together the following March.

In her book *Poor Pearl, Poor Girl!: The Murdered-Girl Stereotype in Ballad and Newspaper*, Anne B. Cohen traces the evolution of Pearl's media portrayal. At first, the papers painted her as "a woman of the town" who wore clothing "of the cheapest description." Her other traits went unmentioned, except to say she appeared to be "of the lower class." Once the coroner's discovery of her pregnancy came to light, however, journalists seized the opportunity to capture public sympathy. Comments on her dress fell away, and she became "a young and trusting girl, whose only offense was having loved too well." A doctor in attendance at her medical examination told the paper, "The girl, in my opinion, was from the country and was comparatively innocent." Pearl was buried in Greencastle. The case had become such a news sensation that her tombstone has been chipped down to its base, apparently by "relic hunters" seeking a literal piece of her story.

The ballads informed by early newspaper reports are equally reductive. Unsurprisingly for an American-born ballad, the fact of the attempted abortion is absent from almost all known variants of the song. Pearl's decapitation is also frequently omitted, perhaps less as a matter of censure than to present Pearl as the quintessential murdered-sweetheart Beheading was, as W. K. McNeil wrote in his 1987 book *Southern Folk Ballads*, "not among the methods by which girls traditionally meet their end in murdered-girl songs"—and so it was ignored. The practice of "editing" a factual report to please a particular audience was, of course, neither new nor unusual, but in the case of "Pearl Bryan" variants, it was particularly flagrant. For example, one popular version is a transparent reworking of an older American ballad called "The Jealous Lover," in which an envious man stabs or drowns a woman as she begs for her life (a classic murdered-sweetheart formulation). Clearly, the balladeers—like some journalists—were less interested in reporting facts than in twisting Pearl's story to suit their purposes.

Like other ballads of this subgenre, "Pearl Bryan" was wielded as a cautionary tale for women. An influential rendition recorded by Vernon Dalhart (under the alias Al Craver) in 1926 opens with the pointed address, "Now ladies, if you listen . . ." and ends, "Take heed! Take heed!" Describing men as essentially "unjust" and untrustworthy, Dalhart goes on to invoke the all-too-familiar "boys will be boys" idea, relieving men of any accountability while implying that women are responsible for the violence done to them. "Believe it, girls; don't let this be your lot," he sings, where "let" is the operative word.

But at the same time, it is the murdered-sweetheart's blind trust that drives her appeal. Cohen points out that many of the usual epithets for murdered-sweethearts are applied to Pearl Bryan. Called a "young girl," "fair maiden," and "darling girl," Pearl is rendered as passive, accommodating, and naive. One variant reveals this by dwelling on an image of Pearl leaving her "happy home" hand in hand with her lover, not realizing that "the grip she carried . . . would hide her head away."

To be a proper young lady, it seems—one deserving of sympathy—is to be two opposing things at once: on the one hand, pure and trusting of heart, and on the other, ever-skeptical of men's intentions. But if the murdered-sweetheart archetype teaches us anything, it's that neither a woman's innocence nor her worldliness will prevent men's violence. Only men can do that.

Under the name The Three Kentucky Serenaders, The North Carolina Ramblers recorded a version in 1927 called "Pearl Bryant," featuring Pearl in her role as the naive ingenue led astray and Scott Jackson as her fiendish killer. Like many variants, the ballad excludes any facts of the case in favor of a boilerplate murdered-sweetheart narrative and all the attending motifs: birds, flowers, and an extended description of Pearl's pleas and lamentations. Despite its clear ambition as a cautionary tale, this variant does not open with the customary warning to "young girls" or "ladies."

"Pearl Bryant"

The Three Kentucky Serenaders, 1927 record single

Way down in Yander's Valley,
Where the flowers fade and bloom,
Our own Pearl Bryant is sleeping,
In a cold and silent tomb.

She died not brokenhearted,
Nor by disease she fell,
But in one instant parted,
From the home she loved so well.

One night when the moon shone brightly,
The stars were shining too,
Then to her cottage window,
Her jealous lover drew.

"Come, Pearl, and let's go wander,
Down in the wilds so gay,
Come, love, and let us ponder
Upon our wedding day."

Deep, deep into the valley,
He led his Pearl so dear,
Said she in sorrow only,
"Well I am wandering here."

"The way grows dark and dreary,
And I'm afraid to stay.
Besides, I'm worn and weary,
I must retrace my way.

"What have I done, Scott Jackson,
That you should take my life?
I've always loved you dearly,
And would have been your wife.

"Farewell, my loving parents,
My face you'll never see more,
How long you'll wait my coming,
To a little cottage door.

"Farewell, my darling sister,
My peaceful, happy home,
Farewell, my dear old schoolmates,
With you no more I'll roam."

When the birds were singing sweetly,
Their bright and joyous song,
They found Pearl's Bryant's body,
On the cold and silent ground.

CHILD OWLET

The noblewoman Lady Erskine sits in her chamber sewing a gift for her nephew, Child Owlet, whom she asks to "cuckold" her husband, Lord Ronald. When he vehemently denies her advances, she cuts or stabs herself "below her green stay's cord" and runs to her husband to accuse Child Owlet of attempted rape. The boy flees but is caught, and the available punishments are carefully considered. Ultimately, Lord Ronald decides that Child Owlet will be drawn and quartered (i.e., tethered to horses and torn limb from limb), and the song often ends with a description of the execution's gory aftermath.

While female villains are not unheard of in balladry of this era, this aunt's attempted seduction (and indirect murder) of her young nephew is, for lack of a better phrase, a bit odd. Less odd, however, is the fact that she leaves the killing itself to her husband, implying that a woman's most useful weapon was not her physical power or even her social position but her clever incitement of men's violence on her behalf. While it's unclear whether Lady Erskine simply injures herself or in fact takes her own life, the story admits that, for a woman to kill, she too will need to bleed.

A "Childe Owlet" appears in Scottish collector Peter Buchan's 1828 text, *Ancient Ballads and Songs of the North of Scotland,* and Francis Child includes a nearly identical version in *The English and Scottish Popular Ballads, Part IX,* published in 1894. Per Buchan's notes, Lady Erskine may have been "the daughter of one of the Earls of Marr [*sic*]," a province in northeastern Scotland; however, her precise historical identity (and those of "Lord Ronald" and "Child Owlet") remains unclear. It is also possible that her story is not hers at all but derived from earlier narrative traditions. In Greek myth, for example, Theseus's queen, Phaedra, falls in love with Hippolytus, her stepson. He rejects Phaedra, and she kills herself, leaving a note for Theseus in which she accuses Hippolytus of having tried to rape her. Theseus uses a wish granted him by Poseidon to summon a giant bull from the sea. The monster spooks Hippolytus's horses, who drag him to his death.

"Child Owlet" is unique in that the first known audio recording of the tune was not released until 1976, when Ewan MacColl and Peggy Seeger included "Chylde Owlet" on their album *No Tyme Lyke the Present.* Most modern versions, including MacColl and Seeger's rendition, differ little from the Buchan and Child ballads, suggesting the song may have gone dormant for some time before being rediscovered.

Classified as Child 291, "Child Owlet" is one of the only ballads in Francis Child's collection that does not list any variants. Child lists two sources for the ballad: the 1828 text of the Scottish collector Peter Buchan and the 1832 manuscript of his correspondent and fellow collector, William Motherwell. In the former, Buchan suggests that "Lady Erskine" may refer to the daughter of one of the Earls of "Marr" (Mar). Although neither Buchan nor Motherwell nor Child offers an origin year for the song, its antiquated language suggests that it may be very old indeed. The Earldom of Mar belonged to various Erskines between the fifteenth century and the time of Buchan's book's publication in 1828.

"Child Owlet"

Collected by Francis Child in *The English and Scottish Popular Ballads, Part IX*

Lady Erskine sits in her chamber,
Sewing at her silken seam,
A chain of gold for Childe Owlet,
As he goes out and in.

But it fell ance upon a day
She unto him did say,
Ye must cuckold Lord Ronald,
 For a' his lands and ley.

"O cease! forbid, madam," he says,
"That this shoud eer be done!
 How would I cuckold Lord Ronald,
And me his sister's son?"

Then she's ta'en out a little penknife,
That lay below her bed,
Put it below her green stay's cord,
Which made her body bleed.

Then in it came him Lord Ronald,
Hearing his lady's moan;
"What blood is this, my dear," he says,
"That sparks on the fire-stone?"

"Young Childe Owlet, your sister's son,
Is now gane frae my bower;
If I hadna been a good woman,
I'd been Childe Owlet's whore."

Then he has taen him Childe Owlet,
Laid him in prison strong,
And all his men a council held
How they woud work him wrong.

Some said they woud Childe Owlet hang,
Some said they woud him burn;
Some said they woud have Childe Owlet
Between wild horses torn.

"There are horses in your stables stand
Can run right speedilie,
And ye will to your stable go,
And wile out four for me."

They put a foal to ilka foot,
And ane to ilka hand,
And sent them down to Darling muir,
As fast as they coud gang.

There was not a kow in Darling muir,
Nor ae piece o a rind,
But drappit o Child Owlet's blude
And pieces o his skin.

There was not a kow in Darling muir,
Nor ae piece o a rash,
But drappit o Childe Owlet's blude
And pieces o his flesh.

FRANKIE AND JOHNNY

Considered the most commercially successful murder ballad of all time, "Frankie and Johnny" has been recorded by more than 250 musicians, including Sam Cooke, Johnny Cash, Bob Dylan, and Stevie Wonder, to name a few. It has also inspired films and plays. But the song's popularity came at great cost to its real-life protagonist, Frankie Baker, who, despite being cleared of the murder the ballad describes, never lived it down.

In 1899, Frankie Baker was a twenty-two-year-old sex worker living in St. Louis's Chestnut Valley—a primarily Black community and hub of ragtime music and culture. Allen Britt (called "Albert") was her seventeen-year-old boyfriend and, many believe, her pimp. A sharp dresser and well-regarded saloon pianist in the neighborhood, Albert lived with Frankie in a rooming house on Targee Street, but he was two-timing her with a woman named Alice Pryor.

In the early morning hours of October 15, 1899, according to Frankie's testimony, Albert stumbled into her room in a rage after an evening spent with Alice. Threatening to leave Frankie, he threw an oil lamp before brandishing a knife. Fearing for her life, Frankie grabbed the .38 pistol she'd stashed under her pillow and shot Albert in the stomach. He died several days later in the hospital.

Frankie's trial took place the following month. In addition to the events of that night, she testified to Albert's history of domestic violence, claiming he had beaten her badly just a few days before his death. The judge ruled that Frankie had acted in self-defense, and she was found not guilty. By the time the verdict was handed down, however, oral tradition had seized control of Frankie's story, and a famous murder ballad was born.

Just weeks after the shooting, Bill Dooley, a St. Louis–based ragtime pianist, began performing a song called "Frankie Killed Allen." A few years later, in 1904, ragtime composer Hughie Cannon set Dooley's tune to new lyrics, publishing sheet music for a ballad called "He Done Me Wrong." By 1912, the vaudeville performers Frank and Bert Leighton had adapted the tune, changing Albert's name to "Johnny" and thus coining "Frankie and Johnny." Regardless of the characters' names, these early ballads emphasize that Frankie shot Albert (Johnny) because he had "done her wrong." In them, Frankie is rarely condemned—she is even called a "good girl"—but according to the song, the "wrong" done to Frankie is Johnny's two-timing, not his violent abuse, and she kills him out of jealousy rather than self-defense.

The ballads caused quite a stir, and Frankie was regularly stalked and harassed. Tired of this treatment, she left St. Louis in 1900 or 1901, settling first in Omaha, Nebraska, and later in Portland, Oregon. She opened a shoeshine business, but "Frankie and Johnny" was popular across the country, and it continued to haunt her. In the late 1920s and early '30s, Mississippi John Hurt and Gene Autry, among others, released popular renditions; Hollywood, too, began to capitalize on the story, casting white actors in the title roles. In *She Done Him Wrong* (1933), Mae West portrays Frankie alongside Cary Grant as Johnny, and in 1936, Republic Pictures released *Frankie and Johnnie,* starring Helen Morgan and Chester Morris. Though the films borrowed little from the ballad apart from the titular characters' names, they only made life harder for the real Frankie Baker. Of course, the movie studios did not compensate Frankie for the use of her name or story, so she sued them—and lost.

Frankie Baker saw her life reduced to a single misrepresented event. She endured decades of harassment, not to mention near-constant reminders of a traumatic past. Unsurprisingly, her mental health suffered greatly, and she was eventually admitted to Oregon's Multnomah County Poor Farm. She died in 1952, at the age of seventy-five.

Female killers aren't all that uncommon in murder ballads, and their motives are as varied as their circumstances. However, the story of Frankie Baker, and of "Frankie and Johnny," is noteworthy. Rarely in real life do we see a woman—especially a Black woman—walk free after killing a dangerous man in self-defense. Yet what followed is all too common: the woman's erasure from her own story as it was co-opted for entertainment.

Although the real Frankie Baker suffered due to her story's notoriety, balladeers did not generally seek to shame or demean her in the way they did, say, Delia Green of "Delia's Gone" (see page 30). Nevertheless, they presented an incomplete portrait—one in which a woman's self-defense is recast as petty revenge.

In 1928, the Delta blues musician Mississippi John Hurt released his version of the ballad titled, aptly, "Frankie." Like most other variants in the tradition, Hurt's suggests that Frankie shot Albert because he'd "done [her] wrong"—meaning he'd cheated on her with another woman. Hurt's song implies that Frankie's actions were, if not fully justified, deeply understandable given Albert's infidelity. He pictures Frankie exiting the courtroom alongside the judge, who tells her, "You're gonna be justified."

"Frankie"

Mississippi John Hurt, 1928 record single

Frankie was a good girl
Everybody know
She paid one hundred dollars
For Albert's suit of clothes
He's her man, and he did her wrong

Frankie went down to the corner saloon
Didn't go to be gone long
She peeped through the keyhole of the door
Spied Albert in Alice's arms
He's my man, and he done me wrong

Frankie called Albert
Albert says, "I don't hear"
If you don't come to the woman you love
Gonna haul you out of here
You's my man and you done me wrong

Frankie shot old Albert
And she shot him three or four times
Said, "Stroll back out the smoke of my gun
Let me see this Albert dying
He's my man and he done me wrong"

Frankie and the judge walked down the stand
Walked out side to side
The judge says to Frankie,
"You're gonna be justified
For killing a man, and he done you wrong"

Dark was the night
Cold was on the ground
The last word I heard Frankie say,
"I done laid old Albert down
He's my man, and he done me wrong"

I ain't gon' tell no stories
And I ain't gon' tell no lies
Well, Albert passed 'bout an hour ago
With a girl they call Alice Fry
He's your man, and he done you wrong

ROSE CONNOLEY

In many ways, "Rose Connoley" is a near-perfect fictional representative of the "murdered-sweetheart" sub-genre. The story follows the usual course: a woman meets her lover in a secluded place—this time a willow garden—where he gives her poison wine, stabs her, and drops her in the river. We learn that the killer's father had promised to bail him out of jail, but he fails to do so and must watch his son be hanged.

In typical fashion, the ballad is sung from the point of view of the killer as he faces the gallows with remorse. Motive, when given in the subgenre, is usually limited to out-of-wedlock pregnancy or the man's desire to be free of an inconvenient relationship, but neither of these is explicitly cited here. In fact, little mention is made of the killer's motive, although in some variants he expresses a version of the old "devil made me do it" excuse. If the song deviates meaningfully from the murdered-sweetheart mold, it is in the focus of the killer's remorse. While he does speak fondly of his victim, calling her a "poor little woman" and "pretty little miss," Rose's killer seems less concerned with her loss than his own foolishness. In other words, he regrets not his crime but the fact that he was caught.

While some initially thought "Rose Connoley" to have originated in America, the scholar D. K. Wilgus argued for its Irish origins, citing an air (the term for an interchangeable melody used in folk music) by the same title collected in 1811 in the north of Ireland by the Irish folklorist Edward Bunting. In his 1979 article "'Rose Connoley': An Irish Ballad" for *The Journal of American Folklore*, Wilgus wrote that the song's isolation to the Appalachian region in America was another clue to its provenance: "It is as if an Irish local song never popularized on broadsides was spread by a single Irish peddler on his travels through Appalachia." While the Bunting air did not include lyrics, in 1983, the folk music historian Donal O'Sullivan and musician and academic Mícheál Ó Súilleabháin supported Wilgus's theory by reuniting the Bunting melody with a lyric fragment found in his manuscripts from the same time. The tune was first collected in America in West Virginia in 1915, then again in 1917, and then in Virginia and North Carolina in 1918. In 1939, the folklorists Anne and Frank Warner recorded another notable Appalachian variant in Sugar Grove, North Carolina, from banjoist Frank Proffitt.

The first audio recording of the song was a 1928 track titled "Rose Conley" by G. B. Grayson and Henry Whitter. More American recordings followed: the country singers Wade Mainer and Zeke Morris released a version in 1937, and Charlie Monroe's 1947 recording helped establish "Down in the Willow Garden"— an alternate title—as a bluegrass standard. Since then, artists such as The Everly Brothers, Art Garfunkel, and, more recently, Nick Cave and the Bad Seeds, Shakey Graves, and Bon Iver have all contributed to the tradition. The lyrics have shifted over the course of the song's recorded life, but the continued use of the name "Rose Connoley" maintains the Irish connection.

The lyrics of Grayson and Whitter's 1928 recording reflect the narrative structure and motifs typical of the American variants. The "devil" is not explicitly mentioned, but the second half of the song tells us that the killer's father had promised to bail him out if he were to kill Rose, implying some serious premeditation. This is a common thread within the American lineage, as is the father's failure in this endeavor and subsequent weeping as he watches his son "upon the scaffold high."

"Rose Conley"

G. B. Grayson and Henry Whitter, 1928 record single

Down in the willow garden
Where me and my love did meet,
O there we sit a-courting,
My love dropped off to sleep.

I had a bottle of the burglar's wine,
Which my true love did not know,
And there I poisoned my old true love
Down under the bank below.

(Spoken: *Poor little woman*)

I drew my sabre through her,
Which was a bloody knife.
I threw her in the river,
Which was a dreadful sight.

My father always taught me
That money would set me free,
If I'd murder that pretty little miss,
Whose name was Rose Connoley.

He's sitting now in his own cottage door
A-wiping his weeping eyes,
A-looking at his own dear son
Upon the scaffold high.

My race is run beneath the sun,
Though hell's now waiting for me.
I did murder that pretty little miss,
Whose name is Rose Connoley.

KNOXVILLE GIRL

A brutal scene unfolds as a man and woman go walking by the river. Seemingly out of nowhere, the man picks up a stick and knocks the unsuspecting woman down. She begs for her life, but he proceeds to beat her to death. He then takes her by her "golden curls" and throws her body in the river, saying:

Go there, go there, you Knoxville girl,
With the dark and rolling eyes,
Go there, go there, you Knoxville girl,
You'll never be my bride.

Typical of a "sweetheart" murder, this one is motivated by the killer's apparent desire to avoid marriage. Although ballads of this type often state or imply that the would-be bride is pregnant, "Knoxville Girl" and its variants never do. In some versions, the murderer faces the gallows with remorse, and in others, in a scene reminiscent of "Lizie Wan" (see page 51), the killer attempts to hide what he's done, telling his worried mother that he's covered in blood due to "bleeding at [his] nose."

While "Knoxville Girl" is generally thought to be a fictional ballad, it has been linked by some scholars to a pair of real-life murders occurring more than two hundred years apart: that of Anne Nichols in Shrewsbury, England, in 1684, and that of Mary Lula Noel in Pineville, Missouri, in 1892.

On February 20, 1684, British clergyman Philip Henry wrote in his diary about a murder that had occurred on "Sabb. day ye 10" (believed to be Sunday, February 10, 1684). A pregnant woman had been killed by a miller—the father of her child—in the nearby town of Shrewsbury. Sometime before 1688, the diarist and ballad collector Samuel Pepys added a ballad titled "The Bloody Miller" to his collection, noting that it was "a true and just Account of one Francis Cooper of Ho[g]stow near Shrewsbury, who was a Miller's Servant" and who "most wickedly and barbarously murdered" his lover of two years, Anne Nichols, who was pregnant by him and under pressure from her father to marry.

"The Bloody Miller" is narrated from the perspective of the killer (Cooper), who gives a woeful account of murdering his pregnant lover (Nichols) by cutting her mouth "from ear to ear" and stabbing her in the head. While the narrator doesn't quite use the nosebleed excuse, he does say that he denied his crime until, in court, "the blood . . . ran from [his] nose"—perhaps due to stress, or, more poetically, to signal his guilt. While Pepys's narrator refers to his victim only as "a maid," an important eighteenth-century descendant of this ballad titled "The Berkshire Tragedy" calls her an "Oxford lass" and has her beaten with a stick and dragged by her hair to the river—details that further link this seventeenth-century ballad to the song we call "Knoxville Girl" in the US.

Several variants of both "The Bloody Miller" and "The Berkshire Tragedy" circulated in England in the eighteenth century, when British ballads were traveling en masse to America. While it's unclear which variant first crossed the Atlantic, it must have done so before 1829, when a broadside ballad called "The Lexington Miller" was printed in Boston. Thought to be a reduced and retold adaptation of "The Berkshire Tragedy," "The Lexington Miller" seems to have kicked off a string of variants in which the song's geography changed as singers personalized the lyrics. Among these were the Tennessean "Knoxville Girl" and, later, the Texan "Waco Girl."

That might have been the whole story of this ballad's lineage—an interesting but relatively uneventful migration from England to Appalachia—but for the 1892 murder of Mary Lula Noel. Ms. Noel, called "Lula," lived in Pineville, a small town in the Missouri Ozarks, with her father, W. H. Noel. In December of 1892, she visited her sister and brother-in-law, a Mr. and Mrs. Holly, on their farm just across Elk River. A young man named William Simmons—Lula's boyfriend, according to some sources—came to visit the Hollys. On the evening of Friday, December 9, the group made plans to cross Elk River the next morning to see the Noel patriarch. Simmons was invited but declined, claiming he planned to catch the train back to Joplin. Lula offered to stay at the farm with Simmons until he left; then, if the river was safe to cross, she would join the others. If the river was too high, however, she planned to stay with relatives nearby.

The river was indeed high that day, and Lula didn't turn up at her family's home. Believing she was safe with relatives, the Hollys stayed on with Mr. Noel for a few more days. Come Monday, however, Lula's relatives across the river confirmed that they had not seen her, and the family began to worry. After a week, they conducted a large, organized search, and Lula's body was found in Elk River, her clothing caught on a willow branch.

Before the big search, when Simmons was confronted in Joplin, he suggested that

Lula may have drowned herself, but this was later disproven by the state of Lula's corpse. Her lungs contained no water, indicating she had died before entering the river. In his 1897 book, *Illustrated History of McDonald County, Missouri: From the Earliest Settlement to the Present Time,* Judge J. A. Sturges wrote that Lula's neck had been broken and her face was bruised "as though a hand had been placed over her mouth to stifle her screams." What's more, a pair of tracks—a man's and a woman's—were found leading from the Hollys' house to the river's edge. Simmons was arrested, jailed in nearby Neosho to avoid a lynching, and tried for first-degree murder in May of 1893. With the jury hung, Simmons's charge was reduced to second degree-murder, of which he was convicted.

In 1927, the folklorist Vance Randolph collected a song titled "The Noel Girl" from a Mrs. Lee Stevens of White Rock, Missouri. Although the song is set in Pineville, where Lula Noel was murdered, it contains several elements in common with "The Bloody Miller" and its variants, right down to the killer's alleged nosebleed. Around the same time, a musician named Arthur Tanner recorded a very similar ballad in which the events described in "The Noel Girl" are set in Knoxville, Tennessee. Titled "Knoxville Girl," the song calls its killer "Willie," perhaps in reference to William

Simmons—and most later variants go on to preserve the name.

Now we can see that the story of "Knoxville Girl" is both interesting and eventful indeed, having roots in fiction as well as two historical—and eerily similar—murders, half a world and two centuries removed. "Knoxville Girl" remains the most common American adaptation, having been recorded by The Louvin Brothers, Nick Cave and the Bad Seeds, and many others. Though neither Anne Nichols nor Lula Noel lived or was killed in Knoxville, that is just as well. At the end of the day, the "Knoxville Girl" could be either or neither of them. She could be any of us, in any "town you all know well."

Arthur Tanner's 1925 recording includes motifs common across "Knoxville Girl" variants and their predecessors, including the couple's "evening walk," the "stick" as bludgeon, the woman's pleas for mercy, her watery grave, and the killer's lie about a nosebleed. Recorded by over fifty artists, including The Louvin Brothers, and, more recently, The Lemonheads, Nick Cave and the Bad Seeds, and Okkervil River, the song remains a mainstay of the American ballad tradition.

"The Knoxville Girl"

Arthur Tanner, 1925 record single

A little girl in Knoxville, a town you all know well
Every Sunday evening, out in her home, I'd dwell
We went to take an evening walk about a mile from town
I picked a stick up off the ground and knocked that fair girl down

She fell upon her bended knees, for mercy she did cry
"Willy, dear, don't kill me here, I'm unprepared to die"
She never spoke another word, just beat her more and more
Until the ground around her within her blood did flow

I took her by those golden curls, I drug her 'round and 'round
I throwed her in the river that flows through Knoxville town
Go there, go there, you Knoxville girl with the dark and rolling eyes
Go there, go there, you Knoxville girl, you'll never be my bride

I started back to Knoxville, got there about midnight
And Mama, she was worried, was awful in a fright
"My son, my son, what have you done to bloody your clothes so?"
The answer I gave Mother was bleeding at my nose

I called for me a candle to light myself to bed
I called for me a handkerchief to bind my aching head
I rolled and tumbled the whole night long, was trouble there for me
Flames of hell around my bed and in my eyes could see

Carried me to the Knoxville jail, they locked me in a cell
My friends all tried to clear me, but none could pay my bill
Her sister swore my life away, she knew without a doubt
Because I was the same young man that carried her sister out

THE DEATH OF QUEEN JANE

"The Death of Queen Jane" may seem an odd inclusion here; although the titular queen dies tragically, she is not a murder victim. But all art forms have iterations that branch away from the central trunk—they move in a different direction, yet they share roots with the more obvious examples of the form. Though "The Death of Queen Jane" is in many ways an outlier, the "sweet flower" at its center is not unlike the beautiful, dead maidens found elsewhere in the murder ballad tradition.

Typically, the victim in a nonfictional ballad is known only for their murder and its subsequent legacy in song. The dead woman at the heart of this ballad, however, is likely Jane Seymour—third wife of King Henry VIII of England. Despite her royalty, Jane's story was subject to the same romantic impulses found in most murder ballads. In fact, her status may have only increased the likelihood of inaccuracies.

The ballad story, which remains stable across variants, is as follows: Queen Jane is having a difficult labor and begs for surgery to save the child. King Henry at first refuses to sacrifice Jane, but the surgery becomes necessary, and a cesarean section is performed. Although the baby is saved, Jane dies, and instead of celebrating the birth of a new heir to the throne, the public grieves for their queen.

Although the facts of Jane Seymour's death have long been contested, most modern historians accept that the queen died of an infection following a vaginal birth. According to Alastair Vannan's account in his article, "The Death of Queen Jane: Ballad, History, and Propaganda," Jane went into labor on or around October 9, 1537, and gave birth to Prince Edward on October 12. Exhausted after the three-day labor, she made plans for the official announcement while still in bed, and King Henry arranged for celebrations in honor of his new son and heir. A few days later, Edward was christened, and Jane watched the proceedings and welcomed guests from an anteroom, having barely rested since the birth.

The churching ceremony—a customary blessing of the mother after childbirth—took place on October 16. The next day, however, Jane developed a fever and quickly became delirious. She began to deteriorate so quickly that last rites were administered. Her condition improved and worsened several times over the next few days, but by the evening of October 24, she took a terrible turn, becoming nearly unresponsive. Jane died that night.

Many historians now believe that the cesarean rumor was put forward to the public as Catholic propaganda. Henry VIII famously rejected the Catholic church, establishing the Church of England so he could divorce his first wife, Catherine of Aragon—on the grounds that she failed to provide him a male heir—and marry Anne Boleyn. Nicolas Sander (or Sanders), a Catholic priest and a vocal supporter of the church, provided one of the earliest reports of Jane's death, in which he told the dramatic tale of Henry and his impossible choice. Sander claimed Henry chose his son over Jane because, as scholar Alastair Vannan puts it, "he could easily find another wife" (which, propaganda or not, history has shown to be very true). The accuracy of Sander's report was not challenged until the early eighteenth century, when in 1721, English clergyman John Strype accused Sander of fabricating the story of the surgery as, according to Vannan, "a malicious attack on Henry, motivated by [Sander's] Catholic loyalties."

Vannan writes that variants of "The Death of Queen Jane" can be grouped into two strands. The first contains the descendants of a printed composition called "The Wofull Death of Queene Jane, Wife to King Henry the Eight: And How King Edward Was Cut out of His Mother's Belly." First published in a 1612 song anthology titled *A Crowne Garland of Goulden Roses* and credited to a Richard Johnson, the ballad may have existed as a broadside as early as 1592. The second strand is that of oral tradition. While unpublished ballads likely circulated from the time of Jane's death and Sander's report, the earliest documented variant was transcribed in 1776 by Thomas Barnard, dean of Derry, from his mother's memory. Additional variants have been collected across Great Britain and the US, a testament, perhaps, to the fame of the ballad's central characters, but also the story's humanity. Passed from one individual to another, each one moved by its sadness, the tale makes no mention of politics but focuses on Jane's struggle and Henry's tortured choice. It was sometimes even sung in the first person, adding to the sense of its deep relatability at a time when many listeners would have experienced a similar tragedy.

In 1917, Cecil Sharp collected "The Death of Queen Jane" from a Mrs. Kate Thomas of Lee County, Kentucky, printing it in his book *English Folk Songs from the*

Southern Appalachians, vol. 1. Although the ballad is remarkably stable, one can spot minor differences in vocabulary and phrasing, as well as small creative embellishments, across variants. In this account, Henry's dramatic arrival on horseback, the fictional length of Jane's labor ("six weeks and some more"), and King Henry's weeping "till his hands were wrung sore," are all such embellishments. Henry's reference to his wife as a flower in this version is also of note, as the Jane-as-flower motif is common. In some variants, Henry expands on the metaphor, saying: "If I lose the flower of England, I shall lose the branch too."

"The Death of Queen Jane"

Sung in 1917 by Mrs. Kate Thomas of Lee County, Kentucky.

Collected by Cecil Sharp in *English Folk Songs from the Southern Appalachians*, vol. 1.

Queen Jane was in labor
Six weeks and some more;
The women grew wearied
And the midwife gave o'er.

O women, kind women,
I take you to be,
Just pierce my right side open
And save my baby.

O no, said the women,
That could never be,
I'll send for King Henry
In the time of your need.

King Henry was sent for
On horse-back and speed;
King Henry he reached her
In the hour of her need.

King Henry he come
And he bent o'er the bed:
What's the matter with my flower
Makes her eyes look so red?

O Henry, kind Henry,
Pray listen to me,
And pierce my right side open
And save my baby.

O no, said King Henry,
That could never be,

I would lose my sweet flower
To save my baby.

Queen Jane she turned over
And fell in a swound,
And her side was pierced open
And the baby was found.

The baby were christened
All on the next day;
But its mother's poor body
Lay cold as the clay.

So black was the mourning,
So yellow was the bed,
So costly was the white robe
Queen Jane was wrapped in.

Six men wore their robes,
Four carrying her along;
King Henry followed after
With his black mourning on.

King Henry he wept
Till his hands were wrung sore.
The flower of England
Will flourish no more.

And the baby were christened
All on the next day,
And its mother's poor body
Lying moldering away.

STAGOLEE

At its most basic, the story of Lee Shelton is the true story of a Black man who got into a fight, shot someone at a bar, and died in prison. But the story of "Stagolee" is that of how an archetypal "badman" ballad became a symbol of Black masculinity and the fight for agency within systems of oppression, transforming the titular hero from a mere character into a legend.

On Christmas night, 1895, William "Billy" Lyons and his friend Henry Crump walked up to Bill Curtis's saloon at the corner of Morgan and Eleventh Streets in an area of St. Louis, Missouri, known as the "Bloody Third" district. Upon entering the bar, Lyons ordered a beer and turned with the rest of the patrons to the door as Shelton, a carriage driver and pimp known at the time as "Stack Lee," entered. He walked in looking sharp in a pair of so-called St. Louis flats with mirrors on the toes that, according to Cecil Brown's account in *Stagolee Shot Billy*, "caught the electric light hanging overhead and sent sparkles upward." Shelton donned "dove-colored spats" atop his shoes, gray-striped pants, and a black box-back coat over a red velvet vest and yellow embroidered shirt. "His left hand," Brown writes, "clutched the gold head of an ebony walking cane," and he wore "a high-roller, milk-white Stetson."

Shelton sat down at the bar with Lyons, and all seemed friendly until a political argument began and escalated. The two men began, as Brown puts it, "to exchange blows by striking each other's hats." When Shelton eventually damaged Lyons's derby, Lyons snatched the Stetson from Shelton's head, refusing to return it. Shelton then brandished a revolver and struck Lyons over the head with it—but to no avail. As Shelton threatened to shoot unless Lyons returned his hat, Lyons retrieved a knife from his coat. That's when, according to the testimony of two eye-witnesses, Shelton shot Lyons. Per Brown's account, he then "snatched his hat from Lyons's hand, put it on his head, and walked out." Shelton returned to his home nearby, where he was arrested in the wee hours of the following morning.

Shelton's first trial ended in a hung jury. Not much is known of the second trial, but it must have resulted in a guilty verdict, because on October 7, 1897, Shelton entered the Missouri State Penitentiary to serve a sentence of twenty-five years. He was paroled in 1909 but found himself back in prison on new charges in 1911. He died in the prison hospital in Jefferson City, Missouri, in 1912.

"Stagolee" has its roots in the ragtime tradition, of which St. Louis was a major hub. From there, the song traveled both north and south, emerging as an instrumental jazz tune in cities like Chicago and New Orleans, and as a folk ballad in the rural South. Along its more rural trajectory, the song hopped from singer to singer, getting quite cozy in the warmth of oral tradition, reproducing as countless narrative variants and cementing the character of "Stack" as a true folk hero for the Black population—the baddest of all the "badmen." The tune became especially popular as a work song in some of the South's most oppressive prisons. In fact, one of the oldest of the preserved rural recordings features Lonnie Robertson, an inmate at Parchman Farm—another name for the notorious Mississippi State Penitentiary—who performed for Alan Lomax in April 1936.

Stagolee as the archetypal "badman" performs a significant role in the examination and expression of Black masculinity. In Houston A. Baker Jr.'s *Long Black Song: Essays in Black American Literature and Culture*, the writer states that "Stackolee represents the badman hero who stands outside the law." For Black men struggling under the crush and cruelty of Jim Crow laws in the early twentieth century, whose lives were in grave danger if they so much as looked at a white woman in a way she didn't like, a song about a Black figure who not only has agency but is at times too powerful in his "badness" to even fear white authority provided—as the scholar George M. Eberhart put it in a 1996 article for *Popular Music and Society*—"a primeval cry in the wilderness by an emasculated class trapped in a dystopia orchestrated by whites."

Unlike in murdered-sweetheart ballads, where killers express remorse as they face the gallows, or revenant ballads, where they come face-to-face with their victims, the killers in "badman" ballads are presented with pity and respect, if not outright admiration. In Stagolee's case, his "badness" was linked to his masculinity, and in the context of the Civil Rights Movement, "self-assertive manhood" became, as Martin Luther King Jr. famously expressed, essential to Black liberation. Singers often took Stagolee's badness to the limit, claiming he was born of the devil, or was at least in league with him. The scholar James P. Hauser wrote in his essay "Stagger Lee: The Story of the Black Badman, the Stetson Hat, and the Ultimate Rock and Roll Record" that in some variants, Stagolee descends to hell after his death or execution, "but is so 'bad' that he takes control of the devil's kingdom and turns it into his own badman's paradise." In a 2021 article, Hauser posits that the Stetson hat, acting as a status symbol for Black men at the turn of the twentieth-century, is emblematic of Black masculinity, and "Stagolee and Billy's fight for possession of it could have been symbolic of the black man's fight for manhood." Hauser further theorizes that Billy Lyons became a stand-in for the systems of oppression created by whites. It is believed that Lyons worked on the levee, but he came from a family of status—his brother-in-law was supposedly one of the wealthiest Black men in St. Louis—so it is also believed that his role on the levee was what Hauser refers to as "black muscle." Lyons was responsible for controlling the other Black workers, and by taking on that role, he helped to "redirect the anger of the brutally treated laborers away from the white bosses and towards other black men." Hauser's interpretation sees Lyons as a proxy for white authority, so that "in doing battle with [him]," Stagolee symbolically fights (and defeats) "the white system of power."

During the first half of the twentieth century, white musicians had their way with Shelton's story, but the song didn't achieve widespread popularity until the 1950s and '60s, when, against the backdrop of the Civil Rights Movement, it was reclaimed by a number of Black musicians. The first records to feature Stagolee were put out by white dance bands, such as Fred Waring's Pennsylvanians and Frank Westphal and His Orchestra. There were some early recordings by Black musicians, such as one by Mississippi John Hurt in 1928, but it was Lloyd Price's 1957 hit "Stagger Lee" that put the song on the mainstream map and helped Stagolee become a galvanizing symbol of the fight for civil rights, finding his way into the hearts and minds of activists.

Well-loved covers by The Isley Brothers, James Brown, and Wilson Pickett followed in the 1960s, and at the same time, a version of the "Stagolee" ballad circulated among the Black community in the form of a toast—a rhythmic, chanted oration made of rhyming couplets in which the speaker identifies as the hero and boasts of his deeds. According to Cecil Brown, Black Panther Party cofounder Bobby Seale was known to perform the Stagolee toast at social gatherings. He even went so far as to name his son, Malik Nkrumah Stagolee Seale, after its titular hero. The Jamaican rocksteady/reggae band The Rulers was also inspired by Stagolee's legend, and in 1967 released "Wrong Emboyo," later adapted as "Wrong 'Em Boyo" by The Clash—with a few lyrical additions of their own—on their album *London Calling*. Bob Dylan, Beck, Taj Mahal, the Grateful Dead, and many others also contributed to the tradition, but the best-known variants remain those recorded by two Black musicians some thirty years apart: Mississippi John Hurt's "Stack O'Lee Blues" and Lloyd Price's "Stagger Lee."

Titled "Original Stack O' Lee Blues," the following variant released by Long "Cleve" Reed and Little Harvey Hull in 1927 sets the events of Lee Shelton's story in Chicago rather than St. Louis and demonstrates that, despite his long career as a bona fide hero, Stagolee was not always thought of as such. The Stagolee-as-bully theme is also found in Mississippi John Hurt's version from the following year, but it became much less common as the song evolved with the twentieth century. In contrast to versions where Stagolee symbolically battles the evils of white supremacy, Reed and Hull's interpretation paints him as viciously cruel and depicts Lyons as a true innocent who begs his killer to think of his wife and two children and spare his life. Reed and Hull do refer to Stagolee as a "bad man," but it seems they meant it in the literal sense.

"Original Stack O' Lee Blues"

Long "Cleve" Reed and Little Harvey Hull, 1927 record single

Stack O' Lee was a bully
He bullied all his life
Well, he bullied through Chicago town
With a ten-cent pocketknife
Then it's ol' Stack O' Lee

Stack said to Billy,
"How can it be?
You'll 'rest a man just as bad as me
But you won't 'rest Stack O' Lee"
Then it's ol' Stack O'Lee

(Spoken: *Ol' bad man*)

Stack said to Billy,
"Don't you take my life
Well, I ain't got not but two little childrens
And a darlin' lovin' wife"
Then it's ol' Stack O' Lee

"One is a boy
And the other one is a girl"
"Well, you may see your children again
But it'll be in another world"

Then it's ol' Stack O' Lee
Standin' on the corner
Well, I didn't mean no harm
Well, that policeman caught me
Well, he grabbed me by my arm
Then it's ol' Stack O' Lee

Stack O' Lee and Billy
Had a noble fight
Well Stack O' Lee killed Billy Lyon
One cold dark soggy night
Then it's ol' Stack O' Lee

(Spoken: *Oh, play it, boys*)

Standin' on the hilltop
The dogs begin to bark
Well, it wasn't nothin' but Stack O' Lee
Come creeping in the dark
Then it's ol' Stack O' Lee

ALICE MITCHELL AND FREDDY WARD

Alice Mitchell and Freda Ward met and fell in love as teenagers at the Higbee School for Young Ladies in Memphis, Tennessee. When Freda's family moved eighty miles up the Mississippi River to the town of Golddust, the pair conducted a secret relationship through correspondence and lengthy visits. Alice asked Freda to marry her once, and then twice more in as many letters. Freda said yes, and they hatched a plan. Alice would cut her hair, dress as a man, maybe even grow a little mustache, and go by the name of Alvin J. Ward. Alvin and Freda would elope to St. Louis, where they'd live as husband and wife.

Alvin, please be perfectly happy when you marry me. for I am true to you, and always will be forever

~ Freda

In July of 1891, however, Freda's eldest sister Ada discovered the pair's letters. Freda confessed everything and was subsequently forced to cut off all contact with Alice. Months passed during which a confused and devastated Alice grew increasingly depressed. In January of 1892, when Alice was nineteen and Freda was seventeen, Freda returned to Memphis to stay with a family friend, but she did not initially contact Alice. On January 18, she finally wrote to her: "I love you now and always will, but I have been forbidden to speak to you and I have to obey. . . . If I have done you any harm or caused you any trouble, I humbly beg your forgiveness." She ended the letter: "We go back to Golddust this evening."

Perhaps clinging to a last sliver of hope, Alice visited the Memphis docks that night, only to find that no boat was scheduled to depart. Her hope turned to rage as she realized Freda had deceived her. Alice eventually discovered that Freda would depart Memphis about a week later. On the appointed day, she stole her father's straight razor and set out in her family's horse-drawn wagon. Spotting Freda and her sister Jo as they headed for the waterfront, Alice tied up the horses, pushed through the crowds, and swung at Freda's neck with the straight razor. "You dirty dog!" Jo reportedly shrieked, lunging at Alice with her umbrella. Alice cut Jo across the collarbone while Freda, bleeding from her neck, fled toward the boat. "You'll hang for this!" Jo yelled after Alice. "I don't care if I'm hung!" Alice called back, catching up with Freda. "I want to die anyhow!" With that, Alice cut Freda again, this time slicing the width of her throat. Freda fell to the ground. As she bled to death, Alice sprinted from the scene. She was arrested an hour later at her parents' home.

The trial lasted ten days and resulted in Alice's acquittal due to insanity. Her lawyers seized on a popular strategy at the time, citing their client's dislike of needlework and other traditionally feminine activities to prove she was "mentally wrong." Even so, they carefully avoided discussing her sexuality. Likewise, the public largely ignored evidence of Alice's romance with Freda. Instead, they were painted as romantic competitors in pursuit of the same men. In one version of this story, a jealous Alice attempted to disfigure her beautiful rival with a razor, accidentally cutting her throat. In another, a love triangle involving a mysterious man prompted the murder. Despite the gossip, Alice made her motivations clear, testifying in court that she killed Freda to, in a way, keep her all to herself.

Alice was committed to the Western State Hospital for the Insane in Bolivar, Tennessee, where she lived for six years until her death at the age of twenty-five. While the hospital issued no cause of death, newspapers reported that Alice had died of tuberculosis, and this was generally accepted. Decades later, however, in 1930, one of her lawyers told Memphis's *Commercial Appeal* that Alice "had taken her own life by jumping into a water tank on top of the building."

At the time of Freda's murder and Alice's trial, homosexuality was poorly understood by the general public and, in most spaces, considered deviant— evidence of disease. Although Alice Mitchell may well have suffered from a legitimate psychiatric illness, it was her love for Freda that proved her a madwoman and sealed her fate. The circumstances of Alice's death, like those of her crime, were not unknowable, and yet they remain the subjects of rumor and speculation. The truth may rest with Alice herself, who is buried in Elmwood Cemetery—just a quarter mile from Freda.

"Alice Mitchell and Freddy Ward" is a jealous-lover ballad, and perhaps the only one of its time in which killer and victim are both women. Despite the headlining murder at its center, only two recorded versions of the ballad are accessible today, both of which date to the early 1960s and are preserved by the John Quincy Wolf Folklore Collection at Lyon College in Batesville, Arkansas. One variant, recorded by Dr. Wolf in 1960, comes from a Mrs. Grace Hastings of Memphis, who claims to have learned the song from her mother, allegedly a friend of Freda Ward. Another, recorded in 1962, comes by way of Mrs. Myron Scruggs, also of Memphis, who heard the song from her aunt.

The two preserved variants are similar, but only Mrs. Hastings's lyrics address Alice's motive directly. In keeping with the rumors of the 1890s, the song suggests Alice killed "Freddy" not because she wanted her to herself but because they both loved the same man. In the Scruggs version, no male love interest is invented; instead, the chorus warns: "Don't fool with a girl with a razor; she'll cut you every time." Scruggs doesn't specify how Freda "fool[ed] with" Alice, but her lyrics may contain a whisper of the truth—that the two women were lovers, and that Alice's actions, however heinous, had nothing to do with her desire for a man.

"Alice Mitchell and Freddy Ward"

Sung in 1960 by Mrs. Grace Hastings of Memphis, Tennessee.
Collected by Dr. John Quincy Wolf.

You all have heard of Freddy Ward,
Who lived many miles from town.
While walking down the stone pavement,
Alice Mitchell cut her down.

She says she killed her because she loved her,
But love was not the thing,
For Alice and Freddy both loved the same man,
And she taken her life for him.

They put her on an eastbound train,
With arms strong tightly bound down.
And every town that she would pass through,
You could hear those people say:

"There goes that Alice Mitchell,
With arms strong tightly bound down,
For the crime she did in Memphis,
She's bound for Bolivar now.

"And they won't do anything to her—
She has two of the best lawyers in town—
But if they served Alice Mitchell right,
They would simply cut her down."

YOUNG HUNTING

The song that eventually became a popular Nick Cave and the Bad Seeds track called "Henry Lee" began its life as a Scottish ballad. "Young Hunting" tells the story of murder by a jealous lover, but this time, that lover is a woman, and her victim is a man. Details vary, as they often do across variants, but the ballad begins with our protagonist, Young Hunting, declining a woman's advances, saying there is another woman he loves more. It is unclear whether these two already know one another, but regardless, the woman is deeply offended by this rejection and so horribly envious that she stabs the man to death.

This is where the narrative becomes unstable across the variants and what happens next becomes convoluted. She might throw him in a river or well. She might gather the women of the town to help her hide the body, which they do without question. Some older variants include the motif of "the bleeding corpse," a popular supernatural device in early modern literature. Used famously in Shakespeare's *Richard III*, a corpse's wound begins bleeding afresh when its murderer is near. Francis Child's B variant of "Young Hunting" describes this memorably:

O white, white war his wounds washen,
As white as a linen clout;

But as the traitor she cam near,
His wounds they gushit out.

In his book *The English Traditional Ballad: Theory, Method, and Practice,* scholar David Atkinson writes that there are several supernatural motifs that serve to reveal the identity of the murderer in older versions of "Young Hunting." In addition to the bleeding corpse, which is present in other variants within the Child collection, some versions have the people looking for Young Hunting set lit candles afloat on the river. The candles burn brighter as they float over the body, revealing its location. The magic candles and bleeding corpse appear together in at least one of the Child variants, but others include just one or the other, or neither. Further revelatory magic is found in some variants where the murderous lady frames her servant. The townspeople attempt to burn the girl at the stake, but the fire does not harm her, as it can only burn the guilty woman. But by far the most common supernatural tattletale is the talking bird.

Once the woman has disposed of the body, and before she is caught, she argues with a bird who has witnessed everything. She attempts to convince the creature to fly down to her, telling it in some variants that she has a lovely golden cage waiting for it at home, but the bird refuses, as in this 1916 Kentuckian variant:

I won't fly down, I won't fly down,
And sit upon your knee;
A girl who would murder her own true love
I'm sure would murder me.

The woman threatens the bird, saying she would shoot it through the heart if she had her bow and arrow. "Who cares I for your bow and arrow?" the bird replies in a 1914 variant collected in Georgia. In another, sourced two years later in Virginia, it then threatens to tell everyone what it saw: "I'd take a flight and fly, fly away, and tune my voice to sing."

In 1987, W. K. McNeil theorized that the ballad traveled directly to America from Scotland, "without leaving much, if any, trace in Britain." Somewhere along that route, however, the name "Young Hunting" was largely lost. While it's unclear how the ballad came to be called either "Henry Lee" or "Love Henry," some scholars have pointed to the bleeding corpse trope (shared with *Richard III*) as a possible source. In the play, it is the corpse of King Henry VI that bleeds when Richard—Henry's killer—approaches.

While Nick Cave and PJ Harvey's sultry 1996 duet is perhaps the best-loved recording in circulation, many came before and have been made since. Blues musician Dick Justice made the earliest known recording in 1929. In 1962, Peggy, Penny, and Barbara Seeger recorded a rendition, as did Judy Henske in 1963. Thirty years later, Bob Dylan joined in with "Love Henry" just before Nick Cave's "Henry Lee" was released.

In 1916, British folklorist Cecil Sharp collected a variant by the old Scottish title from a Mrs. Jane Gentry of Hot Springs, North Carolina. It includes the typical narrative structure: the woman's proposition, the rejection, the murder, the hiding of the body (in this case, without the help of other women), and the confrontation with the talking bird. In this version, Young Hunting mentions his wife in "Old Scotchee," perhaps reflecting the variant's American position, looking back toward its home country of Scotland.

"Young Hunting"

Sung in 1916 by Mrs. Jane Gentry of Hot Springs, North Carolina.

Collected by Cecil Sharp in *English Folk Songs from the Southern Appalachians*, vol. 1.

Come in, come in, my pretty little boy,
And stay this night with me;
For I have got of the very best
And I will give it up to thee.

I can't come in, I won't come in
And stay this night with thee.
For I have a wife in old Scotchee
This night a-looking for me.

She did have a little penknife,
It was both keen and sharp,
She gave him a deathlike blow
And pierced him through the heart.

She picked him up all in her arms,
Being very active and strong.
And she throwed him into an old dry well
About sixty feet.

One day she was setting in her father's parlor door,
Thinking of no harm,
She saw a bird and a pretty little bird
All among the leaves so green.

Come down, come down, my pretty little bird,
And parley on my knee.
I'm afeard you'd rob me of my life
Like you did the poor Scotchee.

I wish I had my bow and arrow,
My arrow and my string;
I'd shoot you through your tender little heart,
For you never no more could sing.

I wish you had your bow and arrow,
Your arrow and your string;
I'd fly away to the Heavens so high,
Where I could for ever more sing.

LAMKIN

"Lamkin" is, as John DeWitt Niles noted in his 1977 article "Lamkin: The Motivation of Horror," a "puzzling ballad." *Puzzling* is a good word for it, as is *unwieldy*: the name of the killer has seemingly infinite spellings and origins; the motive for murder may be supernatural and ritualistic, an act of revenge, or simple depraved cruelty; a mostly unnamed nurse or servant may or may not be his accomplice; and a number of side characters sneak in and out of variants and narrative arcs. At the end of most of the multitudinous variations, however, a woman and her baby are dead, and Lamkin is the killer.

Who is this Lamkin? Aside from a villain with an absurd number of names (Lamkin, Langin, Lomgkin, Lammikin, Bolakin, False Lambkin, Laffin . . .), he is either a mason, a jealous ex, or a garden-variety psychopath.

What did he do? It can be challenging to tell the tale simply, as this ballad's lineage contains endless "corruption[s]," according to Niles, but here is the basic story found in some of its narrative strains: A lord hires a mason to build his castle. The work is done, but the lord does not pay the mason, who becomes enraged and hungry for revenge. With the help of a duplicitous nursemaid, he enters the castle while the lord is away. To lure the lady of the house from her chambers, he "pricks" or stabs her baby. The lady comes down and is seized by the intruder. She offers gold, and sometimes her daughter's hand in marriage, but Lamkin is bloodthirsty and brutally slays the lady. Upon his return, the lord is greeted by the carnage and has Lamkin—and sometimes the nurse—executed.

Before we attempt to untangle this bloody knot of storylines, characters, and motives, some immutable history: A ballad titled "Lammikin" was printed in David Herd's first volume of *Ancient and Modern Scottish Songs, Heroic Ballads, Etc.* in 1776. The year before, Reverend P. Parson of Wye, Kent, England, sent Thomas Percy, the Bishop of Dromore, County Down, a similar ballad. These are the oldest records of the ballad Francis Child would call "Lamkin." The version that became variant A in Child's collection was recorded by the ballad collector Anna Brown and printed in the first volume of Robert Jamieson's *Popular Ballads and Songs: From Tradition, Manuscripts, and Scarce Editions* in 1806. It was then reprinted in many anthologies and became the most well-known version. It maintains one of the most studied elements of the song: the killer's motivation of revenge for nonpayment. This is the only variant that expands the details of the lord's stinginess, gives the wronged mason a chance to express his murderous intentions, and describes the plotting between the "false" nurse and Lamkin before the events unfold.

The wronged mason motif is common throughout the "Lamkin" tradition, but many variants leave Lamkin's motive unsaid, allowing room for speculation. At times, the nurse and the villain are romantically involved and the murder is her idea. Additionally, some scholarship has explored potential supernatural or ritualistic motives. American ballad collector Phillips Barry and folklorist Fannie Hardy Eckstorm sourced a version from a Mrs. Susan M. Harding in Maine in 1934 called "False Linfinn." According to Niles, Barry believed *linfinn* was an Irish term for "the white man who lives by the stream." In Irish folklore, "white man" meant "leper," as Tristram P. Coffin wrote in 1950, indicating that the villain in "Lamkin" is a sickly outcast. Some variants of the ballad mention a silver basin as well, which is significant considering medieval beliefs that one could cure leprosy by collecting blood in such a receptacle. It follows, then, that some scholars would interpret the villain in these variants to be motivated by a desire to cure his horrible disease.

Foundational sacrifice, i.e., sacrifice to ensure a building's strong foundation, has also been suggested by scholars as a motive for the killings. Ninon A. M. Leader investigates this in a study of "Clement Mason," a Hungarian ballad with similar themes. Leader writes, "Where architectural techniques were still primitive, buildings, especially huge ones like castles, bridges and the like, often collapsed while being built or soon after their completion." These catastrophes left the people of the time bewildered, so they blamed the spirits for their misadventures in construction. It naturally followed that the best course of action would be to offer these spirits a human sacrifice. A variety of such rituals have been recorded globally throughout history: people were built into walls while still alive (bringing to mind Edgar Allan Poe's "The Cask of Amontillado"), or, as in the British legend of Vortigern in which a tower's foundation stone is made "wet with the blood of a child," an innocent's blood was mixed with lime to create, as Niles called it, "outstanding mortar." Leader suggests that in certain instances of "Lamkin," the lord fails to provide the required sacrifice, so the mason-villain takes it into his own hands to sacrifice the lord's family, or in some cases, the mason-villain sacrifices *his own* family to the building spirits and kills the lord's family as payback.

Some variants suggest no particular motivation for the murders, essentially rendering Lamkin a depraved and indiscriminate killer. Niles even suggests that the name Lambkin, which is used in several of the variants in Child's collection, is just another word for the devil himself. Niles expands on this, referencing old European beliefs according to which the building of great structures, such as bridges and churches, "may require the assistance of extraordinary powers: a god, a giant, one of the fairy folk, the devil. And these powers must be paid, paid usually not in money or property but in lives."

The devil-as-building-contractor motif is common to a group of Scandinavian legends wherein a supernatural creature, such as a troll or giant, offers construction assistance in exchange for a human sacrifice, unless the person with whom they "contract" can guess the creature's name. Niles refers to these tales originating in Norway and Sweden as "*Finn* legend." A similar tale can be traced to the Scottish Highlands, in which an old man who can't afford to complete his castle strikes a deal with a creature called "a little mannikin," who promises to finish the building if the man agrees to leave with him for a year—unless, of course, he can guess the mannikin's name. Niles theorizes that these overlaps are probably the result of exchanges of lore between Scotsmen and Scandinavian traders or settlers in Scotland and Ireland. Further potential proof of this connection can be found in the names "Linfinn," from Barry's Maine text, and "Lamfin," from a version sourced by the musician and collector John Jacob Niles in Georgia, US, which echo the sounds of *Hin Finn, Fin Fin,* and *Anfinn,* all names associated with the *Finn* legends of Scandinavia.

By the time the ballad was recorded by Percy and Herd in the 1770s, the murders were thought by most to be the result of an unpaid bill rather than monsters or human sacrifice. John Jacob Niles speculates that the extreme reaction of the mason-villain could allude to the resentments of a laboring class who were likely underpaid or occasionally stiffed by lords who'd overstated their wealth. Whatever one believes, the moral of the ballad remains consistent, if hidden. As John DeWitt Niles puts it: "If you strike a bargain with the devil, give him his due—or there will be the devil to pay."

In 1909, in Berkshire, England, Cecil Sharp collected a variant titled "Long Lankin" from a nun of Clewer Parish named Sister Emma. A thorough account containing many of the hallmark themes of "Lamkin"'s tradition, it is also among the variants that ignore the villain-as-mason element, rendering "Long Lankin" a kind of monster. The lord's warnings to "beware of Long Lankin that lives in the moss" and "beware of Long Lankin that lives in the hay" make him sound like a mythical creature of sorts. The nurse here is described as "the false nurse," implying the narrative set-piece of the villain and servant conspiring together. The rest of the ballad plays out like the majority of songs in the tradition, ending with the executions of both Long Lankin, who is "hung on a gibbet so high," and the nurse, who is "burnt in a fire close by."

"Long Lankin"

Sung in 1909 by Sister Emma of Clewer Parish, Berkshire, England.
Collected by Cecil Sharp for the *Journal of the Folk-Song Society*, Vol. 5, No. 18.

Said my lord to my lady, as he mounted his horse:
"Beware of Long Lankin that lives in the moss."

Said my lord to my lady as he rode away:
"Beware of Long Lankin that lives in the hay."

"Let the doors be all bolted and the windows all pinned,
And leave not a hole for a mouse to creep in."

So he kissed his fair lady and he rode away,
And he was in fair London before the head of day.

The doors were all bolted and the windows all pinned,
Except one little window where Long Lankin crept in.

"Where is the lord of this house?" said Long Lankin.
"He's away in fair London," said the false nurse to him.

"Where is the little heir of this house?" said Long Lankin.
"He's asleep in his cradle," said the false nurse to him.

"We'll prick him, we'll prick him all over with a pin,
And that'll make my lady to come down to him."

So he pricked him, he pricked him all over with a pin,
And the nurse held the basin for the blood to flow in.

"O nurse, how you slumber. O nurse, how you sleep.
You leave my little son Johnson to cry and to weep."

"O nurse, how you slumber, O nurse how you snore.
You leave my little son Johnson to cry and to roar."

"I've tried him with an apple, I've tried him with a pear.
Come down, my fair lady, and rock him in your chair."

"I've tried him with milk, I've tried him with pap.
Come down, my fair lady, and rock him in your lap."

"How can I come down, 'tis so late in the night?
There's no fire burning, no candle to give light."

"You have three silver mantles as bright as the sun.
Come down, my fair lady, all by the light of one."

My lady came down the stairs thinking no harm.
Long Lankin stood ready to catch her in his arm.

Her maiden looked out from the turret so high
And she saw her master from London riding by.

"O master, O master, don't lay the blame on me.
'Twas the false nurse and Lankin that killed your fair lady."

Long Lankin was hung on a gibbet so high
And the false nurse was burnt in a fire close by.

THE CRUEL SHIP'S CARPENTER

At first glance, "The Cruel Ship's Carpenter" seems like yet another murdered-sweetheart ballad, another pregnant woman deceived and slain by the father of her child. This ballad, however, affords the victim something our other murdered sweethearts never receive: revenge from beyond the grave.

It begins like all the rest: a woman is made pregnant by a man whom she believes loves her. He promises marriage and takes her on his horse to visit a friend before they can be wed. However, their journey ends not at the altar but a pre-dug grave. She pleads for her life and the life of the baby she carries, but he ignores her, stabbing her in the heart "'til the red blood did flow" and burying her where she will never be found. So many of her sister ballads end here, with a senseless death and perhaps the remorse of the killer as he faces the gallows, but this story continues.

Our villain boards a ship on which he works as a carpenter, but before setting sail, the captain announces that a murderer is among the crew. The crew, including the killer, proclaim their innocence, but as the killer turns to walk away, he is met by the ghost of the woman he just savagely murdered. Her bloody vengeance takes

an array of forms across the variants, but a favorite goes like this:

She stript him and tore him, she tore him in three,
Because he had murdered her baby and she.

The provenance of this ballad can be traced to a British broadside titled "The Gosport Tragedy, or The Perjured Ship's Captain" that dates to around 1750 in London. A very similar broadside was printed in the 1800s in Boston, and more printings followed in both Britain and America throughout that century, sometimes under alternate titles such as "Love and Murder," "Polly's Love," and "The Ghost Song." Eventually, the ballad made its way to the maritime provinces of eastern Canada, appearing as "The Ship's Carpenter" in Kenneth Peacock's 1965 *Songs of the Newfoundland Outports*, vol. 2, and "Pretty Polly" in MacEdward Leach's *Folk Ballads and Songs of the Lower Labrador Coast* (also 1965). A much more widely known title, "Pretty Polly" is generally a shortened version of "The Cruel Ship's Carpenter" in which the supernatural element is removed and the victim is, like a more typical murdered-sweetheart, buried in an unmarked grave. However, in the version collected by Leach from the Labrador coast, we have the full story, including Polly's spectral revenge.

An unusual co-inhabitant of the revenant and murdered-sweetheart genres, "The Cruel Ship's Carpenter" offers a satisfaction normally denied listeners of dead-girl songs. Typically, the murdered sweetheart remains inanimate, forever floating down the river; she doesn't return to tell her story, much less tear her killer to shreds. Despite this, "Pretty Polly" has come to be the ballad's dominant variant, and its best-known lyrics don't feature her vengeful return.

Pete Seeger, Judy Collins, Bob Dylan, and, more recently, Sturgill Simpson have recorded their own renditions of the ballad. Occasionally some of the modern recordings, usually under the title "Ghost Song" or more rarely "The Cruel Ship's Carpenter," retain the proper ending and see the murderous man ruined, but much more often, Polly is left to molder in her grave.

A variant of the ballad set in Worcestershire, England, appears on a British broadside dating to between 1858 and 1885. It contains one of the earliest references to the victim as "Polly"—the name she would come to adopt—and it features the ballad's original narrative in full, including the killer's return to his ship, where he encounters Polly's bloodthirsty ghost.

"Polly's Love; or, The Cruel Ship Carpenter"

English broadside from the Harding collection at the Bodleian Libraries, University of Oxford

In fair Worcester city, in Worcestershire,
A handsome young damsel, she lived there,
A handsome young man he courted her to be his dear,
And he was by trade a ship carpenter.

Now the King wanted seamen to go on the sea,
That caus'd this young damsel to sigh and to say,
O William, O William, don't you go to sea,
Remember the vow that you made to me.

It was early next morning before it was day,
He went to his Polly, these words he did say,
O Polly, O Polly, you must go with me
Before we are married, my friends for to see.

He led her through groves and vallies so deep
And caused this young damsel to sigh and to weep,
O William, O William, you have led me astray,
On purpose my innocent life to betray,

It's true, it's true, these words he did say,
For all the night long I've been digging your grave,
The grave being open, the spade standing by,
Which caus'd this young damsel to sigh and to cry.

O William, O William, O pardon my life,
I never will covet to be your wife,
I will travel the country to set you quite free,
O pardon, O pardon, my baby and me.

No pardon I'll give, there's no time to stand,
So with that he had a knife in his hand,
He stabb'd her heart till the blood it did flow,
Then into the grave her fair body did throw.

He covered her up so safe and secure,
Thinking no one would find her he was sure,
Then he went on board to sail the world round
Before that murder could ever be found.

It was early one morning, before it was day,
The captain came up, these words he did say,
There's a murderer on board, and he it has lately done,
Our ship is in mourning, she cannot sail on.

Then up stepp'd one, indeed it's not me,
Then up stepp'd another, the same he did say,
Then up starts young William, to stamp and to swear,
Indeed it's not me, I vow and declare.

As he was turning from the captain with speed,
He met his Polly, which made his heart to bleed,
She stript him and tore him, she tore him for the three,
Remember young William, my baby and me.

MARROWBONES

An old woman from seemingly many places—Wexford, Dublin, Dover—"loved her old husband dearly, but another man twice as well." When she consults a doctor on how to best blind her spouse, he tells her to "feed him eggs and marrowbone." She takes his advice, serving her husband a plate of marrowbone (sometimes with eggs on the side). The dish delivers on its promise, and, blinded, her distraught husband asks her to help him drown. At the river's bank, she moves to push him into the current, but at the last moment, he steps aside, sending her into the water instead. She pleads for rescue, but he claims he is unable to help her, for he cannot see. He proceeds to use a long pole to push her under the water until she drowns.

Some ballads leave behind a clear trail of breadcrumbs guiding us to their original home, revealing their evolution along the way. Others present as a densely tangled briar of oral tradition, their inception concealed somewhere at its thorny center. This ballad is one of the latter. Cecil Sharp remarked that it is "a very widely known song that, for some reason, has rarely found its way into printed collections in Britain." Instead, it has had a vivid life in the oral tradition, going by many different names, including (but not limited to) "There Was an Old Woman in Our Town," "Marrowbones," "Eggs and Marrowbones," "The Wily Auld Carle," and "The Wife from Kelso." Often, it appeared as "The Old Woman of Wexford" (or Oxford, Slapsadam, Dublin, London . . .), and at times, simply "The Old Woman in Our Town."

While we do not have old broadsides or chapbooks to illuminate this ballad's lineage, we do know that "Marrowbones" is related to a ballad called "Johnny Sands," which also tells of a man who asks his wife to assist in his suicide by drowning. At the river's edge, the man's wife binds his arms with rope, and as she goes to push him in, he moves out of the way, allowing her to fall into the water. When she begs for his help, he says he can do nothing since he is tied up. While some scholars believe "Marrowbones" and "Johnny Sands" to be variants of the same ballad, others claim they may have influenced each other but are distinct. Whatever their relationship, they share a "punchline": a man asks his wife to drown him, yet she ends up drowning instead.

On paper, it all sounds quite horrible, these murderous tricks between husbands and wives, but the ballads are part of the *schwank* ("farce") song subgenre (a category created by German ballad scholars) and are actually intended to be humorous. Rainer Wehse, in his article "Broadside Ballad and Folksong: Oral Tradition versus Literary Tradition," defined a *schwank* song as "a humorous narrative" in which "a dramatic conflict reaches its height toward the end of the tale or song culminating in a point . . . usually the inversion of the initial situation." While most murder ballads seek to impress listeners with tragedy or scandal, one like "Marrowbones" survives because generations of listeners have found it funny and worth passing along without much alteration. This may also explain its popularity in folk song rather than print. Twentieth-century folk revivalists took a particular liking to the tune. Many figures of the movement, especially in Ireland and the UK, recorded renditions, including Frankie Armstrong, and the band Steeleye Span.

another man, the trip to the doctor who prescribes the meal of marrowbones, the blinding of the old man, and his vengeful—and humorous—trick. The song's final stanza, in which the singer threatens to stop singing if he isn't given "some drink," do veer slightly from the song's tradition, but they also evidence its use as entertainment, as in a rowdy bar.

In 1921, Cecil Sharp and Maud Karpeles collected a variant of "Marrowbones" from Thomas Taylor at Ross Workhouse in Herefordshire, England. It is standard to the "Marrowbones" tradition, with lines referring to the old woman's love for

"There Was an Old Woman in Our Town (The Rich Old Lady)"

Sung in 1921 by Thomas Taylor of Herefordshire, England.

Collected by Cecil Sharp and Maud Karpeles in the *Journal of the English Folk Dance and Song Society.*

There was an old woman in our town,
In our town did dwell,
And she loved her husband dearly,
But another man twice as well.

Sing whip she la-rey, tid-i-foo la-rey,
Whip she la-rey O.

Now she went and got six marrow-bones
And she made him suck them all,
And that made the old man blind
Till he couldn't see any at all.

The old man said he'd drown himself
If he could find the way.
The old woman quickly answered:
O I'll show you the way.

She led him to the water
And took him to the brim.
And he said he'd drown himself
If she would push him in.

The old woman she went to give a run
To push the old man in,
And he popped to the one side,
And the woman went tumbling in.

She plunged about in the water
A-thinking she could swim
But the old man went and got a puthering
    prop
And he propped her further in.

So now my song is ended,
You may pen it down in ink.
I won't bother my head to sing any more
If you don't give me some drink.

THE UNQUIET GRAVE

A man or a woman, depending on the variant, vows to sit and weep at the grave of their one true love for a year and a day. After this period of mourning, the dead lover arises from his or her grave, chastising the living for disrupting their eternal rest. The bereaved lover begs their beloved for a final kiss, but the deceased warns that such a kiss would kill the living. The murder in this ballad is barely remarked upon, with many versions stating only that the lost love was "slain."

Most often in revenant ballads, the dead return as phantoms, but "The Unquiet Grave" is somewhat unique in that it describes the physical body of the dead rising from the grave. The Scottish folklorist David Buchan wrote in a 1986 article that the dead in the many variants of "The Unquiet Grave" appear "to help people [. . .] cope with grieving and the dislocations of death."

Many cultures around the world have believed that excessive mourning disturbs the rest of the dead and should be avoided. In an article for *The Journal of the English Folk Dance and Song Society,* Ruth Harvey places "The Unquiet Grave" in a group of ballads emerging from Scandinavia, Germany, and Britain that share this theme. In *"Aage og Else"* ("Aage and Else") from Denmark and *"Sorgens Magt"* ("The Power of Grief") from Sweden, a woman weeps and weeps at the grave of her love. When the dead man rises, annoyed at this disturbance, he tells her that her tears have filled his grave. In the Old Norse tale *"Helgakvida Hundingsbana II"* ("The Second Lay of Helgi Hundingsbane"), the dead Helgi appears to his love Sigrún soaked in blood because, as Harvey writes, "every one of her tears falls heavy and cold, like blood, on his breast as he lies in the grave-mound." Additionally, the German ballad *"Der Vorwirt"* ("The Former Husband") tells of a dead man who entreats his living wife to give him a dry shirt—because his is soaked with her tears.

"The Unquiet Grave" is, according to the American historian and folklorist Arthur Kyle Davis Jr., "a rich repository of antique folklore and popular beliefs," including, among others, one in "magic-tasks." In his 1916 book, *One Hundred English Folksongs,* Cecil Sharp writes of an ancient superstition whereby a maiden's betrothal to a man withstood his death. In the event of her fiancé's demise, the engaged woman would be "compelled to follow [her betrothed] into the spirit world unless she was able to perform certain tasks or solve certain riddles that he propounded." Davis suggests that the "magic-task" motif found in most variants of "The Unquiet Grave" is an echo of this older belief. Sharp's book includes a variant in which a man weeps excessively at the grave of his slain "sweetheart." When the man says he'll leave his love be if he can just have "a kiss from [her] lily-white lips," the dead woman warns him that if he kisses her, "[his] days they won't be long." She then directs him to obtain various unobtainable or "magic" items, such as "water from the desert," "blood from out of a stone," and milk from the breast of a virgin. The implication, it seems, is that no matter how the man may try, he will never get the "one thing that [he] crave[s]"—which is for his love to return to life.

"The Unquiet Grave" does not differ much from version to version, except to swap the gender of the revenant and bereaved. While it is related to ballads from Scandinavia, it seems to be primarily rooted in Britain and, given its narrative stability, likely derives from a primary printed source such as a broadside, though none has been discovered. Francis Child preserved nine variants from Britain and Scotland in his collection, and folklorists such as Cecil Sharp, Lucy E. Broadwood, and Anne G. Gilchrist went on to add more than a dozen new English variants to the tradition. The ballad did not establish itself in North America on the same scale as some others. The earliest known American-sourced variant was collected by Arthur Kyle Davis Jr. from a Mrs. Chaney Smith in Virginia in 1912. Another version and a fragment were sourced in Newfoundland in 1929, and in 1934, the collector John Jacob Niles logged a variant from Kentucky.

"Cold Blows the Wind," a variant of "The Unquiet Grave," was collected by Charlotte Sophia Burne in the English county of Shropshire in the late nineteenth century. In the early 1870s, Burne began working with historian and folklorist Georgina F. Jackson, who had already spent decades in the field studying local folklore and customs. Due to a long illness, Jackson eventually passed her work on to Burne, who was more interested in the folk music of the area, and supplemented Jackson's collection with local songs. One such song was a variant of "The Unquiet Grave" sourced from a Jane Butler of Edgmond, Shropshire. A solid example of the ballad's tradition, it includes the irritated revenant, the living's request for a final kiss, and the dead's assignment of "magic-tasks," which, in this version, include obtaining "a nut from a dungeon deep."

"Cold Blows the Wind"

Sung by Jane Butler of Edgmond, England. Collected by Charlotte Sophia Burne in *Shropshire Folk-Lore: A Sheaf of Gleanings from the Collections of Georgina F. Jackson.*

"Cold blows the wind over my true love,
Cold blow the drops of rain;
I never never had but one true love,
And in Camvil[l]e he was slain."

"I'll do as much for my true love
As any young girl may,
I'll sit and weep down by his grave
For twelve months and one day."

But when twelve months were come and gone,
This young man he arose.
"What makes you weep down by my grave?
I can't take my repose."

"One kiss, one kiss, of your lily-white lips,
One kiss is all I crave;
One kiss, one kiss, of your lily-white lips,
And return back to your grave!"

"My lips they are as cold as my clay,
My breath is heavy and strong,
If thou wast to kiss my lily-white lips,
Thy days would not be long!"

"O don't you remember the garden-grove
Where we was used to walk?
Pluck the finest flower of them all,
'Twill wither to a stalk!"

"Go fetch me a nut from a dungeon deep,
And water from a stone,
And white milk from a maiden's breast
[That babe bare never none]."

["Go dig me a grave both long, wide, and deep,
 (As quickly as you may),
I will lie down in it and take one sleep,
For a twelvemonth and one day!
I will lie down in it and take one sleep,
For twelvemonth and one day!"]

118

NOTABLE RECORDINGS

OMIE WISE

Also called: NAOMI WISE | OMMIE WISE | (LITTLE) OMA WISE | POOR NAOMI | POOR OMIE

1927: Jep Fuller (Vernon Dalhart), "Naomi Wise" (single)

1928: G. B. Grayson, "Ommie Wise" (single)

1959: Shirley Collins, "Omie Wise," *Sweet England*

1964: Doc Watson, "Omie Wise," *Doc Watson*

2006: Kate and Anna McGarrigle with Elvis Costello, "Ommie Wise Part 1 & 2 (What Lewis Did Last . . .)," *The Harry Smith Project: Anthology of American Folk Music Revisited*

2013: Vandaveer, "Omie Wise," *Oh, Willie, Please . . .*

THE CRUEL MOTHER

Also called: THE DUKE'S DAUGHTER'S CRUELTY | THE GREENWOOD SIDE | GREENWOOD SIDEY | DOWN BY THE GREENWOOD SIDEY-O | FINE FLOWERS IN THE VALLEY | THE LADY OF YORK | CARLISLE WALL | THE ROSE O' MALINDIE O | THE LADY FROM LEE

1956: Ewan MacColl, "The Cruel Mother," *The English and Scottish Popular Ballads (The Child Ballads) Volume 4*

1960: Shirley Collins, "The Cruel Mother," *False True Lovers*

1964: Judy Collins, "Cruel Mother," *The Judy Collins Concert*

1967: Joan Baez, "The Greenwood Side," *Joan*

1971: Martin Carthy, "Cruel Mother," *Landfall*

1972: Frankie Armstrong, "The Cruel Mother," *Lovely on the Water*

1977: Peggy Seeger, "Down by the Greenwood Sidey-O," *American Folk Songs for Children*

1989: Steeleye Span, "The Cruel Mother," *Tempted and Tried*

1992: Helen Bonchek Schneyer, "The Cruel Mother," *Somber, Sacred & Silly*

2015: 10,000 Maniacs, "Greenwood Sidey," *Twice Told Tales*

DELIA'S GONE

Also called: DELIA | ONE MORE ROUNDER GONE

1924: Reese Du Pree, "One More Rounder Gone" (single)

1935: Nassau String Band, "Delia Gone," *Deep River of Song: Bahamas 1935,* Volume 2 (released in 2002)

1940: Blind Willie McTell, "Delia," *Blind Willie McTell: 1940* (released in 1965)

1954: Pete Seeger, "Delia's Gone," *The Pete Seeger Sampler*

1958: Harry Belafonte with The Belafonte Singers and Orchestra, conducted by Bob Corman, "Delia's Gone," *Love Is a Gentle Thing*

1960: Pat Boone, "Delia Gone" (single)

1962: Johnny Cash, "Delia's Gone," *The Sound of Johnny Cash*
1969: Waylon Jennings, "Delia's Gone" (single)
1993: Bob Dylan, "Delia," *World Gone Wrong*
1994: Johnny Cash, "Delia's Gone," *American Recordings*

IN THE PINES
Also called: THE LONGEST TRAIN | WHERE DID YOU SLEEP LAST NIGHT? | BLACK GIRL | BLACK GAL | TRUE LOVE TRUE LOVE | LITTLE GIRL
1926: "Dock" Walsh, "In the Pines" (single)
1941: Bill Monroe and His Blue Grass Boys, "In the Pines," *Blue Yodel No. 7*
1944: Lead Belly, "(Black Gal) Where Did You Sleep Last Night?" (single)
1956: The Louvin Brothers, "In the Pines," *Tragic Songs of Life*
1961: Connie Francis, "True Love True Love," *Connie Francis Sings Folk Song Favorites*
1966: Tiny Tim, "Little Girl" (single)
1966: The Grateful Dead, "In the Pines," *The Golden Road (1965-1973)* (released in 2001)
1976: The Carter Family, "In the Pines (The Longest Train I Ever Saw)," *Country's First Family*
1982: Joan Baez, "In the Pines," *Very Early Joan*
1982: Doc Watson, "In the Pines," *Out in the Country*
1993: Nirvana, "Where Did You Sleep Last Night," *MTV Unplugged in New York* (released in 1994)
1994: Dolly Parton, "In the Pines," *Heartsongs: Live from Home*
2016: Loretta Lynn, "In the Pines," *Full Circle*

THE BLOODY GARDENER
Also called: THE BLOODY GARDENER'S CRUELTY | THE SHEPHERD'S DAUGHTER BETRAY'D
1956: A. L. Lloyd, "The Bloody Gardener," *English Street Songs*
1967: Martin Carthy and Dave Swarbrick, "The Bloody Gardener," *Byker Hill*
1988: Arthur Knevett, "The Bloody Gardener," *Mostly Ballads*
2016: Rachel Newton, "The Bloody Gardener," *Here's My Heart Come Take It*
2019: Ruth Barrett, "The Bloody Gardener," *Jane Austen's Sanditon (Original Television Soundtrack)*
2020: Karina Knight, "The Bloody Gardener," *From the Knee*

THE TWA SISTERS
Also called: THE MILLER AND THE KING'S DAUGHTER | (THE) TWO SISTERS | (OH THE DREADFUL) WIND AND RAIN | (THE BONNY) BOWS OF LONDON (TOWN) | MINNORIE | BINNORIE | THE CRUEL SISTER | THE BERKSHIRE TRAGEDY
1956: John Jacob Niles, "The Two Sisters, or The Old Lord by the North Sea," *American Folk and Gambling Songs*

1958: Peggy Seeger, "Two Sisters," *Alan Lomax Presents Folk-Song Saturday Night*
1959: Shirley Collins, "The Berkshire Tragedy," *The Foggy Dew and Other English Songs*
1970: Kilby Snow, "Wind and Rain," *Kilby Snow: Country Songs and Tunes with Autoharp*
1977: Jody Stecher, "Oh the Wind and Rain," *Going Up on the Mountain*
1978: Dan Tate, "Wind and Rain," *Virginia Traditions: Ballads from British Tradition*
1990: Martin Carthy and Dave Swarbrick, "Bows of London," *Life and Limb*
1996: Jerry Garcia and David Grisman, "Dreadful Wind and Rain," *Shady Grove*
2001: Gillian Welch, David Rawlings, and David Steele, "Wind and Rain," *Songcatcher: Music from and Inspired by the Motion Picture*
2006: Tom Waits, "Two Sisters," *Orphans: Brawlers, Bawlers & Bastards*
2015: Okkervil River, "Oh, the Wind and Rain," *Black Sheep Boy (Anniversary Edition)*
2016: Steeleye Span, "Two Sisters," *Dodgy Bastards*

LIZIE WAN
Also called: LIZZIE WAN | LUCY WAN | ROSIE ANNE | FAIR LUCY | FAIR LIZZIE
1967: Martin Carthy, "Lucy Wan," *Byker Hill*
1967: Hedy West, "Lucy Wan," *Ballads*
1997: Frankie Armstrong, "Fair Lizzie," *Till the Grass O'ergrew the Corn*
2003: Kathryn Roberts and Sean Lakeman, "Rosie Anne," *2.*

PEARL BRYAN
Also called: THE JEALOUS LOVER | PEARL BRYANT
1926: Vernon Dalhart (as Jep Fuller), "Pearl Bryan" (single)
1927: The Three Kentucky Serenaders, "Pearl Bryant" (single)
1928: Burnett and Rutherford, "Pearl Bryan" (single)
1965: A. L. Phipps and the Phipps Family, "Pearl Bryan," *Faith, Love and Tragedy*
1965: Doc Hopkins, "Pearl Bryant," *Doc Hopkins* (released in 1971)
2001: The Crooked Jades, "Pearl Bryan/Intro" and "Pearl Bryan/Outro," *Seven Sisters: A Kentucky Portrait* (music from the documentary film)

CHILD OWLET
Also called: CHILDE OWLET | CHYLDE OWLET(T)
1976: Ewan MacColl and Peggy Seeger, "Chylde Owlet," *No Tyme Lyke the Present*
1998: Alistair Hulett and Dave Swarbrick, "Chylde Owlett," *The Cold Grey Light of Dawn*
2004: Steeleye Span, "Child Owlet," *They Called Her Babylon*
2015: Kathryn Roberts and Sean Lakeman, "Child Owlet," *Tomorrow Will Follow Today*

FRANKIE AND JOHNNY
Also called: FRANKIE KILLED ALLEN | FRANKIE AND ALBERT | FRANKIE

1916: The Leighton Brothers, "Frankie and Johnny" (never released)

1928: Mississippi John Hurt, "Frankie" (single)

1929: Gene Autry, "Frankie and Johnny" (single)

1939: Lead Belly, "Frankie and Albert (First Half)" and "Frankie and Albert (Completion)," *Negro Sinful Songs*

1947: Lena Horne with vocal chorus, Phil Moore conducting, "Frankie and Johnny" (single)

1954: Mae West, with quartet and orchestra directed by Sy Oliver, "Frankie and Johnny," *The Fabulous Mae West* (released in 1955)

1956: Sammy Davis Jr., "Frankie and Johnny" (single)

1957: Pete Seeger, "Frankie and Johnny," *American Favorite Ballads*

1959: Louis Armstrong and his orchestra, "Frankie and Johnny," *Satchmo Plays King Oliver*

1961: Sam Cooke, "Frankie and Johnny" (single) (released in 1963)

1965: Elvis Presley, "Frankie and Johnny," *Frankie and Johnny* (original soundtrack album)

1968: Roberta Flack, "Frankie and Johnny," *First Take (50th Anniversary Deluxe Edition)* (released in 2020)

1973: Taj Mahal, "Frankie and Albert," *Oooh So Good 'n Blues*

1992: Bob Dylan, "Frankie & Albert," *Good As I Been to You*

1999: Beth Orton, "Frankie," *The Harry Smith Project: Anthology of American Folk Music Revisited* (released in 2006)

ROSE CONNOLEY

Also called: ROSE CONNOLLY | ROSE CONLEY | (DOWN IN A/THE) WILLOW GARDEN

1927: Grayson and Whitter, "Rose Conley" (single) (released in 1928)

1956: The Kossoy Sisters, "Down in a Willow Garden," *Bowling Green and Other Folk Songs from the Southern Mountains*

1958: The Everly Brothers, "Down in the Willow Garden," *Songs Our Daddy Taught Us*

1958: Ramblin' Jack Elliott, "In the Willow Garden," *Ramblin' Jack Elliott in London* (released in 1959)

1964: Lester Flatt and Earl Scruggs, "Rose Conelly," *The Versatile Flatt & Scruggs: Pickin' Strummin' and Singin'* (released in 1965)

1973: Art Garfunkel, "Down in the Willow Garden," *Angel Clare*

1995: Nick Cave and the Bad Seeds, "The Willow Garden," *Where the Wild Roses Grow*

2013: Vandaveer, "Down in the Willow Garden," *Oh, Willie, Please . . .*

2017: Lankum, "Willow Garden," *Between the Earth and Sky*

KNOXVILLE GIRL

Also called: (THE) OXFORD/WEXFORD/WACO GIRL | THE BERKSHIRE TRAGEDY | THE CRUEL MILLER | THE LEXINGTON MILLER/MURDER | NEVER LET THE DEVIL GET THE UPPER HAND OF YOU

1925: Arthur Tanner, "The Knoxville Girl" (single)

1937: The Carter Family, "Never Let the Devil Get the Upper Hand of You" (single) (released in 1938)
1956: The Louvin Brothers, "Knoxville Girl," *Tragic Songs of Life*
1981: Charlie Feathers, "Knoxville Girl," *Long Time Ago: Rare and Unissued Recordings, Volume 3* (released in 2008)
1996: Nick Cave and the Bad Seeds, "Knoxville Girl," *Henry Lee*
1996: The Lemonheads, "Knoxville Girl," *Car Button Cloth*
2006: Charlie Louvin feat. Will Oldham, "Knoxville Girl," *Charlie Louvin* (released in 2007)

THE DEATH OF QUEEN JANE
Also called: THE WOFULL DEATH OF QUEENE JANE | QUEEN JANE
1941: John Jacob Niles, "The Death of Queen Jane," *American Folk Lore, Volume 3*
1962: Peggy Seeger, "The Death of Queen Jane," *A Song for You and Me*
1964: Joan Baez, "The Death of Queen Jane," *5*
1980: Joan Sprung, "The Death of Queen Jane," *Pictures to My Mind*
1992: Helen Bonchek Schneyer, "Queen Jane," *Somber, Sacred & Silly*
2013: Oscar Isaac, "The Death of Queen Jane," *Inside Llewyn Davis: Original Soundtrack Recording*
2015: 10,000 Maniacs, "Death of Queen Jane," *Twice Told Tales*

STAGOLEE
Also called: STAGGER LEE | STACK O' LEE BLUES | STACKOLEE | STACKALEE | STACK A LEE | STAG-O-LEE | WRONG 'EM BOYO
1923: Waring's Pennsylvanians, "Stack O' Lee Blues" (single)
1926: "Ma" Rainey with Her Georgia Band, "Stack O' Lee Blues" (single)
1927: Frank Hutchison, "Stackalee" (single)
1928: Mississippi John Hurt, "Stack O'Lee Blues" (single) (released in 1929)
1928: The Washingtonians, "Stack O' Lee Blues" (single)
1956: Woody Guthrie, "Stagolee," *Bound for Glory: The Songs and Stories of Woody Guthrie*
1957: Lloyd Price, "Stagger Lee," *Presenting Lloyd Price*
1958: Pete Seeger, "Stagolee," *American Favorite Ballads, Volume 2*
1960: Bill Haley and His Comets, "Stagger Lee," *Bill Haley and His Comets*
1963: The Isley Brothers, "Stagger Lee," *Twisting and Shouting*
1967: Wilson Pickett, "Stag-O-Lee," (single)
1967: The Rulers, "Wrong Emboyo" (single)
1978: Grateful Dead, "Stagger Lee," *Shakedown Street*
1979: The Clash, "Wrong 'Em Boyo," *London Calling*
1993: Bob Dylan, "Stack A Lee," *World Gone Wrong*
1996: Nick Cave and the Bad Seeds, "Stagger Lee," *Murder Ballads*
2001: Beck, "Stagolee," *Avalon Blues: A Tribute to the Music of Mississippi John Hurt*

ALICE MITCHELL AND FREDDY WARD
1960: Mrs. Grace Hastings, "Alice Mitchell and Freddy Ward," part of the John Quincy Wolf Folklore Collection
1962: Mrs. Myron Scruggs, "Alice Mitchell and Freddy Ward," part of the John Quincy Wolf Folklore Collection

YOUNG HUNTING
Also called: LOVE HENRY | HENRY LEE | EARL RICHARD | THE FALSE LADY | SONG OF A LOST HUNTER | YOUNG REDIN
1929: Dick Justice, "Henry Lee" (single)
1957: Logan English, "Love Henry," *Kentucky Folk Songs and Ballads*
1962: Peggy Seeger with Barbara and Penny Seeger, "Henry Lee," *The Three Sisters*
1963: Judy Henske, "Love Henry," *Judy Henske*
1993: Bob Dylan, "Love Henry," *World Gone Wrong*
1996: Nick Cave and the Bad Seeds featuring PJ Harvey, "Henry Lee," *Murder Ballads*
2002: Ralph Stanley, "Henry Lee," *Ralph Stanley*
2010: Crooked Still, "Henry Lee," *Some Strange Country*
2013: Vandaveer, "Henry Lee," *Oh, Willie, Please . . .*

LAMKIN
Also called: LAMBKIN | LONG LANKIN | LONG LONGKIN | BALANKIN | LAMBERT LINKIN | RANKIN | LAMMIKIN | CRUEL LINCOLN | BEAULAMPKIN | FALSE LINFINN
1956: A. L. Lloyd, "Long Lankin," *The English and Scottish Popular Ballads, Volume III*
1968: Hedy West, "Beaulampkin," *Ballads*
1968: Martin Carthy and Dave Swarbrick, "Long Lankin," *But Two Came By*
1975: Steeleye Span, "Long Lankin," *Commoners Crown*
2016: Shirley Collins, "Cruel Lincoln," *Lodestar*

THE CRUEL SHIP'S CARPENTER
Also called: THE GOSPORT TRAGEDY | THE PERJURED SHIP CARPENTER | PRETTY POLLY | THE GHOST SHIP | THE GHOST SONG | POLLY'S LOVE | LOVE AND MURDER
1926: Lester McFarland and Robert A. Gardner, "Pretty Polly" (single)
1950: Burl Ives, "Pretty Polly," *More Folksongs*
1957: Pete Seeger, "Pretty Polly," *American Ballads*
1961: Hedy West, "Pretty Polly," *New Folks*
1966: A. L. Lloyd, "Pretty Polly," *The Bird in the Bush: Traditional Erotic Songs*
1967: Ewan MacColl, "The Ghost Ship," *The Long Harvest, Record Two*
1968: The Byrds, "Pretty Polly," *The Byrds* (released in 1990)
1968: Judy Collins, "Pretty Polly," *Who Knows Where the Time Goes*

1977: Mike Waterson, "The Cruel Ship's Carpenter," *Mike Waterson*
2013: Vandaveer, "Pretty Polly," *Oh, Willie, Please . . .*
2014: Béla Fleck and Abigail Washburn, "Pretty Polly," *Béla Fleck & Abigail Washburn*
2019: Steeleye Span, "The Cruel Ship's Carpenter," *Est'd 1969*

MARROWBONES
Also called: EGGS AND MARROWBONES | THE RICH OLD LADY | TIGERY ORUM | THE WILY AULD CARLE | THE WIFE FROM KELSO | THE OLD WOMAN OF/FROM WEXFORD/OXFORD/SLAPSADAM/DUBLIN/LONDON/OUR TOWN
1964: Harry Cox, "Marrowbones," *Traditional English Love Songs*
1964: Joe Heaney, "The Old Woman of Wexford," *The Road from Connemara* (released in 2000)
1966: A. L. Lloyd, "Tigery Orum," *The Best of A. L. Lloyd*
1971: Steeleye Span, "Marrowbones," *Ten Man Mop or Mr. Reservoir Butler Rides Again*
1973: The Clancy Brothers with Lou Killen, "The Old Woman from Wexford," *Greatest Hits*
1976: Frankie Armstrong, "Marrowbones," *Here's a Health to the Man and the Maid*
2000: Kate Burke and Ruth Hazleton, "Marrowbones," *A Thousand Miles or More*
2017: Jody Stecher and Kate Brislin, "Eggs and Marrowbone," *Big Bend Killing: The Appalachian Ballad Tradition*

THE UNQUIET GRAVE
Also called: COLD BLOWS THE WIND
1956: A. L. Lloyd, "The Unquiet Grave," *The English and Scottish Popular Ballads (The Child Ballads), Volume I*
1959: Shirley Collins, "The Unquiet Grave," *False True Lovers*
1964: Joan Baez, "The Unquiet Grave," *5*
1972: Frankie Armstrong, "The Unquiet Grave," *Lovely on the Water*
1997: Ween, "Cold Blows the Wind," *The Mollusk*
2009: Steeleye Span, "The Unquiet Grave," *Cogs, Wheels and Lovers*

BIBLIOGRAPHY

Abrahams, Roger D., and George Foss. *Anglo-American Folksong Style.* Prentice-Hall, 1968.

Amable, Jody. "The Murder Ballad Was the Original True Crime Podcast." *JSTOR Daily,* January 30, 2021. daily.jstor.org/the-murder-ballad-was-the-original-true-crime-podcast/.

Anderson, John Q. "'The Waco Girl': Another Variant of a British Broadside Ballad." *Western Folklore* 19, no. 2 (1960): 107–18. https://doi.org/10.2307/1496929.

Asch, Moses, Josh Dunson, and Ethel Raim, eds. *Anthology of American Folk Music.* Oak Publications, 1973.

Ashton, John. *A Century of Ballads.* London, 1887.

Atkinson, David. "History, Symbol, and Meaning in 'The Cruel Mother.'" *Folk Music Journal* 6, no. 3 (1992): 359–80. https://www.jstor.org/stable/4522412.

Atkinson, David. "Relationships in Eighteenth-Century Ballads—Negotiation, Ideology, Imagination." *Tautosakos darbai* 59 (June 2020): 48-63. https://doi.org/10.51554/TD.2020.28366.

Atkinson, David. *The English Traditional Ballad: Theory, Method, and Practice.* Routledge, 2002. https://doi.org/10.4324/9781315086675.

Baker, Houston A., Jr. *Long Black Song: Essays in Black American Literature and Culture.* University Press of Virginia, 1972.

Belden, Henry M. *Ballads and Songs Collected by the Missouri Folk-Lore Society.* Second edition. University of Missouri, 1955.

Belden, Henry M., and Arthur Palmer Hudson, eds. *Folk Ballads from North Carolina.* The Frank C. Brown Collection of North Carolina Folklore, edited by Newman Ivey White, vol. 2. Duke University Press, 1952. https://archive.org/details/frankcbrowncolle02fran/.

Blackman, Patrick. "Stagolee—A Digital Compendium: The Classics." *Sing Out!* (blog), March 11, 2013. https://singout.org/stagolee-a-digital-compendium-the-classics/.

Blakemore, Erin. "How U.S. Abortion Laws Went from Nonexistent to Acrimonious." *National Geographic,* April 11, 2023. https://www.nationalgeographic.com/history/article/the-complex-early-history-of-abortion-in-the-united-states.

"The Bloody Gardener's Cruelty; or, The Shepherd's Daughter Betray'd," ca. 1700. *Early English Books Online.* University of Michigan Library Digital Collections. https://name.umdl.umich.edu/B01677.0001.001.

Boatwright, Mody C., Wilson M. Hudson, and Allen Maxwell, eds. *Mesquite and Willow.* Southern Methodist University Press, 1957.

Bolin, Alice. *Dead Girls: Essays on Surviving an American Obsession.* William Morrow, 2018.

Botkin, B. A., ed. *A Treasury of American Folklore: Stories, Ballads, and Traditions of the People.* Crown Publishers, 1944.

Boyke, Molly. "How Murder Ballads Helped." *The Hairpin,* April 19, 2012. https://medium.com/the-hairpin/how-murder-ballads-helped-6dcea15d8bba

Brewster, Paul G., ed. *Ballads and Songs of Indiana.* Indiana University Publications, 1940.

Bronson, Bertrand H. "Mrs. Brown and the Ballad." *California Folklore Quarterly* 4, no. 2 (1945): 129–40. https://doi.org/10.2307/1495675.

Bronson, Bertrand H. "The Interdependence of Ballad Tunes and Texts." *California Folklore Quarterly* 3, no. 3 (1944): 185–207. https://doi.org/10.2307/1495873.

Brown, Cecil. *Stagolee Shot Billy.* Harvard University Press, 2003.

Buchan, David, and Edward D. Ives. "Tale Roles and Revenants: A Morphology of Ghosts." *Western Folklore* 45, no. 2 (1986): 143–60. https://doi.org/10.2307/1500041.

Buchan, Peter. *Ancient Ballads and Songs of the North of Scotland,* vol. 2. Edinburgh, 1828.

Bunting, Edward. *Bunting's Ancient Music of Ireland.* Edited by Donal O'Sullivan and Mícheál Ó Súilleabháin. Cork University Press, 1983.

Burne, Charlotte Sophia, ed. *Shropshire Folk-Lore: A Sheaf of Gleanings from the Collections of Georgina F. Jackson.* London, 1883.

Burt, Olive Woolley. *American Murder Ballads and Their Stories.* Oxford University Press, 1958.

Child, Francis James. *English and Scottish Popular Ballads.* Edited by Helen Child Sargent and George Lyman Kittredge. Houghton Mifflin, 1904.

Coe, Alexis. "A Very Unnatural Crime." *The Toast,* September 6, 2013. https://the-toast.net/2013/09/06/crime-history-alice-mitchell/.

Coe, Alexis. *Alice + Freda Forever: A Murder in Memphis.* Zest Books, 2014.

Coffin, Tristram P. *The British Traditional Ballad in North America.* American Folklore Society, 1950.

Cohen, Anne B. *Poor Pearl, Poor Girl!: The Murdered-Girl Stereotype in Ballad and Newspaper.* University of Texas Press, 1973. https://doi.org/10.7560/764095.

Cohen, Daniel A. "The Beautiful Female Murder Victim: Literary Genres and Courtship Practices in the Origins of a Cultural Motif, 1590–1850." *Journal of Social History* 31, no. 2 (1997): 277–306. http://www.jstor.org/stable/3789940.

Cohen, Norm. *Long Steel Rail: The Railroad in American Folksong.* University of Illinois Press, 1981.

Coppock, Paul. "Memphis' Strangest Love Murder Had All-Girl Cast." *The Commercial Appeal,* September 7, 1930, 49.

Cowdell, Paul. "'I Have Believed in Spirits from That Day unto This': 'The Ghostly Crew,' Ghostlore, and Traditional Song." *Folk Music Journal* 11, no. 4 (2019): 76–98. https://www.jstor.org/stable/44987682.

Cox, John Harrington. *Folk-Songs of the South.* Harvard University Press, 1925.

Craven, Braxton. *Life of Naomi Wise: True Story of a Beautiful Girl, Enacted in Randolph County, N. C., About the Year 1800.* State Library of North Carolina, Government & Heritage Library, n.d. https://archive.org/details/lifeofnaomiwiset00crav/.

Creighton, Helen, ed. *Folksongs from Southern New Brunswick.* National Museums of Canada, 1971.

Dalhart, Vernon. "Pearl Bryan." Columbia Master W 142896 (recorded November 1, 1926). Columbia 15169-D (under pseudonym Al Craver; released August 30, 1927).

Dance, Daryl Cumber. *Shuckin' and Jivin': Folklore from Contemporary Black Americans.* Indiana University Press, 1978.

Davis, Arthur Kyle, Jr., ed. *More Traditional Ballads of Virginia.* University of North Carolina Press, 1960.

Duggan, Lisa. "The Trials of Alice Mitchell: Sensationalism, Sexology, and the Lesbian Subject in Turn-of-the-Century America." *Signs* 18, no. 4 (1993): 791–814. https://www.jstor.org/stable/3174907.

Du Pree, Reese. "One More Rounder Gone." OKeh 8127-B, 1924, record single.

Eberhart, George M. "Stack Lee: The Man, the Music, and the Myth." *Popular Music & Society* 20, no. 1 (1996): 1–70. https://doi.org/10.1080/03007769608591611.

Eckstorm, Fannie Hardy. "Two Maine Texts of 'Lamkin.'" *The Journal of American Folklore* 52, no. 203 (1939): 70–74. https://doi.org/10.2307/536011.

Eddy, Mary O., ed. *Ballads and Songs from Ohio.* Folklore Associates, 1964.

Erbsen, Wayne. *Rural Roots of Bluegrass: Songs, Stories & History.* Native Ground Music, 2003.

Field, Arthur. "Why Is the 'Murdered Girl' So Popular." *Midwest Folklore* 1, no. 2 (1951): 113–19. https://www.jstor.org/stable/4317272.

The Forget Me Not Songster. New York, 1840.

Friedman, Albert B., ed. *The Viking Book of Folk Ballads of the English-Speaking World.* Viking Press, 1956.

Fuller, Jep [Vernon Dalhart] [vocalist]. "Pearl Bryan." Vocalion B 5015, 1927, record single.

Gee, S. "In the Pines: A Guide." *Sing Out!* (blog), March 16, 2015. https://singout.org/pines-guide/.

Gee, S. "Young Hunting (Henry Lee, Love Henry)." *Sing Out!* (blog), January 16, 2012. https://singout.org/young-hunting-henry-lee-love-henry/.

Gerould, Gordon Hall. *The Ballad of Tradition.* Reprinted, Oxford University Press, 1957.

Gilchrist, Anne G. "Lambkin: A Study in Evolution." *Journal of the English Folk Dance and Song Society* 1, no. 1 (1932): 1–17. http://www.jstor.org/stable/4521008.

Grayson, G. B. [vocalist]. "Ommie Wise." Victor 21625-B, 1928, record single.

Grayson, G. B., and Henry Whitter [vocalists]. "Rose Conley." Victor 21625-A, 1928, record single.

Greenleaf, Elizabeth B., and Grace Y. Mansfield, eds. *Ballads and Sea Songs of Newfoundland.* Harvard University Press, 1933.

Gregory, E. David. *Victorian Songhunters: The Recovery and Editing of English Vernacular Ballads and Folk Lyrics, 1820–1883.* Scarecrow Press, 2006.

Greig, Gavin. *Folk-Song in Buchan and Folk-Song of the North-east.* Folklore Associates, 1963.

Hammond, H. E. D., Frank Kidson, Lucy E. Broadwood, et al. "Conventional Ballads." *Journal of the Folk-Song Society* 3, no. 11 (1907): 61–76. https://www.jstor.org/stable/4433914.

Hampton, Joshua. *The Silver Dagger: American Murder Ballads.* Published by the author, 2020.

Harvey, Ruth. "The Unquiet Grave." *Journal of the English Folk Dance and Song Society* 4, no. 2 (1941): 49–66. https://www.jstor.org/stable/4521181.

Hastie, Christina Ruth. "'This Murder Done': Misogyny, Femicide, and Modernity in 19th-Century Appalachian Murder Ballads." Master's thesis, University of Tennessee, 2011. https://trace.tennessee.edu/utk_gradthes/1045.

Hastings, Grace [vocalist]. "Alice Mitchell and Freddy Ward." Recorded August 19, 1960. The John Quincy Wolf Folklore Collection. https://home.lyon.edu/wolfcollection/songs/hastingsalice1245.html.

Hauser, James P. "Stagger Lee: The Story of the Black Badman, the Stetson Hat, and the Ultimate Rock and Roll Record." *The Stagger Lee Files.* https://sites.google.com/site/thestaggerleefiles/original-stagger-lee-essay.

Hauser, Jim. "Stagolee and John Henry: Two Black Freedom Songs?" *The African American Folklorist,* May 17, 2021. https://theafricanamericanfolklorist.com/articles/a-hrefhttptheafricanamericanfolkloristcom20201129twoblackfreedomsongsstagolee-and-john-henry-two-black-freedom-songsa.

Henderson, Kathy, Frankie Armstrong, and Sandra Kerr. *My Song is My Own: 100 Women's Songs.* Pluto Press, 1979.

Henry, Mellinger Edward, ed. *Folk-Songs from the Southern Highlands.* J. J. Augustin Publisher, 1938.

Henry, Mellinger Edward. "Pearl Bryant: An Unpublished Variant of an American Folk Song." *The Journal of American Folklore* 42, no. 165 (1929): 301–3. https://doi.org/10.2307/535041.

Henry, Philip. *Diaries and Letters of Philip Henry, M. A. of Broad Oak, Flintshire.* Edited by Matthew Henry Lee. London, 1882.

Herd, David, ed. *Ancient and Modern Scottish Songs, Heroic Ballads, Etc.,* vol. 1. Second edition. Glasgow, 1869.

Hine, Darlene Clark, and Earnestine Jenkins, eds. *"Manhood Rights": The Construction of Black Male History and Manhood, 1750–1870.* A Question of Manhood: A Reader in U.S. Black Men's History and Masculinity, vol. 1. Indiana University Press, 1999.

Hoffer, Peter C., and N. E. H. Hull. *Murdering Mothers: Infanticide in England and New England 1558–1803.* New York University Press, 1981.

Hurray for the Riff Raff. "The Body Electric." Track 6 on *Small Town Heroes.* ATO Records, 2014.

Hutson, C. Kirk. "'Whackety Whack, Don't Talk Back': The Glorification of Violence Against Females and the Subjugation of Women in Nineteenth-Century Southern Folk Music." *Journal of Women's History* 8, no. 3 (1996): 114–42. https://doi.org/10.1353/jowh.2010.0492.

Jamieson, Robert. *Popular Ballads and Songs, from Tradition, Manuscripts, and Scarce Editions; with Translations of Similar Pieces from the Ancient Danish Language, and A Few Originals by the Editor,* vol. 1. Edinburgh, 1806.

Johnson, Richard. *A Crowne Garland of Goulden Roses.* London, 1612.

Jones, Rhian E., and Eli Davies, eds. *Under My Thumb: Songs That Hate Women and the Women Who Love Them.* Repeater, 2017.

Kader, Emily. "'Rose Connolly' Revisited: Re-Imagining the Irish in Southern Appalachia." *The Journal of American Folklore* 127, no. 506 (2014): 425–47. https://doi.org/10.5406/jamerfolk.127.506.0425.

Kahn, Jamie. "The Song That Inspired Kate Bush to Write a Song about Incest: 'It Was an Area That I Wanted to Explore.'" *Far Out,* March 13, 2022. https://faroutmagazine.co.uk/the-song-that-inspired-kate-bush-to-write-about-incest/.

Karpeles, Maud, ed. *Folk Songs from Newfoundland.* Faber and Faber, 1971.

Kinsley, James, ed. *The Oxford Book of Ballads.* Clarendon Press, 1969.

Kittredge, G. L, ed. "Ballads and Rhymes from Kentucky." *The Journal of American Folklore* 20, no. 79 (1907): 251–77. https://doi.org/10.2307/534475.

Kittredge, G. L. "Ballads and Songs." *The Journal of American Folklore* 30, no. 117 (1917): 283–369. https://doi.org/10.2307/534379.

Laws, G. Malcolm, Jr. *American Balladry from British Broadsides: A Guide for Students and Collectors of Traditional Song.* Bibliographical and Special Series, edited by MacEdward Leach, vol. 8. American Folklore Society, 1957.

Laws, G. Malcolm, Jr. *Native American Balladry: A Descriptive Study and a Bibliographical Syllabus.* Revised edition. American Folklore Society, 1964.

Leach, MacEdward, ed. *The Ballad Book.* Harper, 1955.

Leach, MacEdward. *Folk Ballads and Songs of the Lower Labrador Coast.* National Museum of Canada Anthropological Series, no. 68. Queen's Printer, 1965.

Leader, Ninon A. M. *Hungarian Classical Ballads and Their Folklore.* Cambridge University Press, 1967.

Leisy, James F. *The Folk Song Abecedary: A Living Tradition of Songs, from Ballads to Blues to Bluegrass.* Hawthorn Books, 1966.

Lloyd, A. L. "The Bloody Gardener." Liner notes for *English Street Songs.* Riverside Records RLP 12-614, 1956, record.

Lomax, Alan. "The Cruel Mother." Liner notes for *False True Lovers* by Shirley Collins. Folkways Records FG 3564, 1959, record.

Lomax, Alan. *The Folk Songs of North America: In the English Language.* Doubleday, 1960.

Long-Wilgus, Eleanor R. *Naomi Wise: Creation, Re-Creation, and Continuity in an American Ballad Tradition.* Chapel Hill Press, 2003.

Marcus, Greil. *Mystery Train: Images of America in Rock 'n' Roll Music.* Sixth edition, Plume, 2015.

McCarthy, William B. "William Motherwell as Field Collector." *Folk Music Journal* 5, no. 3 (1987): 295–316. https://www.jstor.org/stable/4522240.

McNeil, W. K., ed. *Southern Mountain Folksongs: Traditional Songs from the Appalachians and the Ozarks.* August House Publishers, 1993.

McNeil, W. K., ed. *Southern Folk Ballads,* vol. 2. August House, 1987.

Miller, D. Q. "Playing a Mean Guitar: The Legacy of Staggerlee in Baldwin and Morrison." In *James Baldwin and Toni Morrison: Comparative Critical and Theoretical Essays,* edited by Lovalerie King and Lynn Orilla Scott. Palgrave Macmillan, 2006.

Milnes, Gerald. "West Virginia's Omie Wise: The Folk Process Unveiled." *Appalachian Journal* 22, no. 4 (1995): 376–89. https://www.jstor.org/stable/40933703.

Miss Cellania [pseud.]. "The Story Behind 'Frankie and Johnny.'" *Mental Floss,* May 3, 2016. https://www.mentalfloss.com/article/78308/story-behind-frankie-and-johnny.

Mississippi John Hurt. "Frankie." OKeh 8560, 1928, record single.

Morgan, Stacy I. *Frankie and Johnny: Race, Gender, and the Work of African American Folklore in 1930s America.* University of Texas Press, 2017. https://doi.org/10.7560/312070.

Motherwell, William. *Minstrelsy: Ancient and Modern, with an Historical Introduction and Notes.* Glasgow, 1827.

Niles, John DeWitt, and Eleanor R. Long. "Context and Loss in Scottish Ballad Tradition." *Western Folklore* 45, no. 2 (1986): 83–109. https://doi.org/10.2307/1500038.

Niles, John DeWitt. "*Lamkin*: The Motivation of Horror." *The Journal of American Folklore* 90, no. 355 (1977): 49–67. https://doi.org/10.2307/539020.

Niles, John Jacob. *The Ballad Book of John Jacob Niles.* Houghton Mifflin, 1961.

Odum, Howard W. "Folk-Song and Folk-Poetry as Found in the Secular Songs of the Southern Negroes (Concluded)." *The Journal of American Folklore* 24, no. 94 (1911): 351–96. https://doi.org/10.2307/534593.

Parker, Harbison. "'The Twa Sisters'—Going Which Way?" *The Journal of American Folklore* 64, no. 254 (1951): 347–60. https://doi.org/10.2307/537003.

Peacock, Kenneth, ed. *Songs of the Newfoundland Outports,* vols. 2–3. National Museum of Canada Anthropological Series, no. 65. Queen's Printer, 1965.

Pepys, Samuel. *The Pepys Ballads,* vol. 3. Edited by Hyder Edward Rollins. Harvard University Press, 1930.

Pollard, Michael. *Discovering English Folksong.* Shire Publications, 1982.

"Polly's Love; or, The Cruel Ship Carpenter." Harding B 11(3056). *Broadside Ballads Online from the Bodleian Libraries.* http://ballads.bodleian.ox.ac.uk/view/sheet/2728.

Purslow, Frank, ed. *Marrow Bones: English Folk Songs from the Hammond and Gardiner Mss.* English Folk Dance and Song Society, 1982.

Randolph, Vance, ed. *Religious Songs and Other Items.* Revised edition. Ozark Folksongs, vol. 2. University of Missouri Press, 1980.

Reed, Long "Cleve," and Little Harvey Hull [vocalists]. "Original Stack O' Lee Blues." Black Patti 8030-B, 1927, record single.

Sander, Nicolas. *Rise and Growth of the Anglican Schism.* Edited by Edward Rishton. Translated by David Lewis. London, 1877.

Scruggs, Myron [vocalist]. "Alice Mitchell and Freddy Ward." Recorded December 13, 1962. The John Quincy Wolf Folklore Collection. https://home.lyon.edu/wolfcollection/songs/scruggsalice1269.html.

Sharp, Cecil J. *English Folk Songs from the Southern Appalachians,* vols. 1–2. Edited by Maud Karpeles. Oxford University Press, 1932.

Sharp, Cecil J., ed. *One Hundred English Folksongs.* Oliver Ditson, 1916.

Sharp, Cecil J., Ralph Vaughan Williams, Frank Kidson, Lucy E. Broadwood, and Anne G. Gilchrist. "Ballads and Songs." *Journal of the Folk-Song Society* 5, no. 18 (1914): 61–94. https://www.jstor.org/stable/4434003.

Sharpe, J. A. *Crime in Early Modern England 1550–1750.* Longman, 1984.

Shields, Hugh. "The Dead Lover's Return in Modern English Ballad Tradition." *Jahrbuch für Volksliedforschung* 17 (1972): 98–114. https://doi.org/10.2307/847175.

Slade, Paul. "'Please Tell Me Where's Her Head': Pearl Bryan in Song and Story." *Planet Slade,* September 2011. http://www.planetslade.com/pdf/PearlBryan.pdf.

Slade, Paul. *Unprepared to Die: America's Greatest Murder Ballads and the True Crime Stories That Inspired Them.* Revised edition. Published by the author, 2021.

Smith, Courtney E. "Delia's Gone: On the Trail of a Folk-Song Ghost." *Majuscule* 11, April 2023. https://majusculelit.com/delias-gone/.

Smith, Courtney E. "What We Lose When We Ignore the Real Roots of Murder Ballads." *Esquire,* July 21, 2021. https://www.esquire.com/entertainment/music/a37078255/history-of-murder-ballads-stagger-lee-true-story/.

"Songs, Hitherto Unpublished, from the Manuscripts of Cecil Sharp." *Journal of the English Folk Dance and Song Society* 8, no. 4 (1959): 197–202. https://www.jstor.org/stable/4521587.

Stecher, Jody. "Oh the Wind and Rain." Track 8 on *Going Up on the Mountain: The Classic First Recordings.* Acoustic Disc ACD-39, 2000, compact disc.

Studio 360. "The Haunting Power of 'In The Pines.'" *Slate,* April 19, 2019. https://slate.com/culture/2019/04/in-the-pines-song-kurt-cobain.html.

Sturges, J. A. *Illustrated History of McDonald County, Missouri: From the Earliest Settlement to the Present Time.* Pineville, Missouri, 1897.

Tanner, Arthur [vocalist]. "The Knoxville Girl." Herwin 75538, 1925, record single.

Terich, Jeff. "'In the Pines'—A Song That Remains Open-Ended after 150 Years." *Treble,* May 11, 2022. https://www.treblezine.com/in-the-pines-song-open-ended-150-years/.

The Three Kentucky Serenaders. "Pearl Bryant." Supertone 9246-B, 1927, record single.

Twitchell, James B. *Forbidden Partners: The Incest Taboo in Modern Culture.* Columbia University Press, 1987.

"Two English Folk Songs." Noted by Tilly Aston. *Journal of the English Folk Dance and Song Society* 1, no. 1 (1932): 52–54. https://www.jstor.org/stable/4521012.

Underwood, Richard H. *CrimeSong: True Crime Stories from Southern Murder Ballads.* Shadelandhouse Modern Press, 2016.

van der Heijden, Manon, Ariadne Schmidt, and Griet Vermeesch. "Illegitimate Parenthood in Early Modern Europe." *The History of the Family* 26, no. 1 (2021): 1–10. https://doi.org/10.1080/10816 02X.2020.1853586.

Vannan, Alastair. "The Death of Queen Jane: Ballad, History, and Propaganda." *Folk Music Journal* 10, no. 3 (2013): 347–69. https://www.jstor.org/stable/43590070.

Walsh, "Dock." "In the Pines." Columbia Records 15094-D, 1926, record single.

Wehse, Rainer. "Broadside Ballad and Folksong: Oral Tradition versus Literary Tradition." *Folklore Forum* 8, no. 1 (1975): 324–34. https://hdl.handle.net/2022/1407.

Wilentz, Sean. "The Sad Song of Delia Green and Cooney Houston." In *The Rose and the Briar: Death, Love and Liberty in the American Ballad,* edited by Sean Wilentz and Greil Marcus. W. W. Norton, 2005.

Wilgus, D. K. "'Rose Connoley': An Irish Ballad." *The Journal of American Folklore* 92, no. 364 (1979): 172–95. https://doi.org/10.2307/539387.

Wilgus, D. K. "Shooting Fish in a Barrel: The Child Ballad in America." *The Journal of American Folklore* 71, no. 280 (1958): 161–64. https://doi.org/10.2307/537690.

Wilhelm, Robert. "Delia's Gone, One More Round." *Murder by Gaslight* (blog), March 21, 2010. https://www.murderbygaslight.com/2010/03/delias-gone-one-more-round.html.

Wilhelm, Robert. "Poor 'Omie: The Murder of Omie Wise." *Murder by Gaslight* (blog), November 2, 2009. https://www.murderbygaslight.com/2009/09/naomi-wise_05.html.

Williams, R. Vaughan, and A. L. Lloyd, eds. *The Penguin Book of English Folk Songs.* Penguin Books, 1959.

Wimberly, Lowry Charles. *Death and Burial Lore in the English and Scottish Popular Ballads.* University of Nebraska Studies in Language, Literature, and Criticism, vol. 8. University of Nebraska, 1927.

Wolfe, Charles K. *Kentucky Country: Folk and Country Music of Kentucky.* University Press of Kentucky, 1982.

Wolford, Leah Jackson. *The Play-Party in Indiana: A Collection of Folk-Songs and Games with Descriptive Introduction, and Correlating Notes.* Indiana Historical Commission, 1916.

Wrightson, Keith. "Infanticide in European History." *Criminal Justice History* 3 (1982): 1–20.

Würzbach, Natascha. *The Rise of the English Street Ballad, 1550–1650.* Translated by Gayna Walls. Cambridge University Press, 1990.

Zierke, Reinhard. "Child Owlet." *Mainly Norfolk: English Folk and Other Good Music.* https://mainlynorfolk.info/steeleye.span/songs/childowlet.html.

RECOMMENDED READING

Alice + Freda Forever: A Murder in Memphis by Alexis Coe

CrimeSong: True Crime Stories from Southern Murder Ballads
by Richard H. Underwood

Dead Girls: Essays on Surviving an American Obsession by Alice Bolin

English Folk Songs from the Southern Appalachians, vols. 1 and 2, by Cecil Sharp

The English Traditional Ballad: Theory, Method, and Practice by David Atkinson

*Frankie and Johnny: Race, Gender, and the Work of African American Folklore in
1930s America* by Stacy I. Morgan

Poor Pearl, Poor Girl: The Murdered Girl Stereotype in Ballad and Newspaper
by Anne B. Cohen

The Rose and the Briar: Death, Love and Liberty in the American Ballad
by Sean Wilentz and Greil Marcus

The Silver Dagger: American Murder Ballads by Joshua Hampton

Stagolee Shot Billy by Cecil Brown

ACKNOWLEDGMENTS

Historically, this is how I do things: I dive headfirst into a new endeavor, then think to myself, once I am in the trenches, *OH NO*—and this book was no different. Now that I am at the end of this process, however, I am very proud of the work I put in, even though I struggled to maintain the belief that I could, in fact, deliver the book I'd been carrying in my mind and heart for over a decade. Luckily, I am surrounded by kind, beautiful people who believed even when I didn't.

To the scholars, folklorists and writers of today and yesterday who opened the portal for me into the rich depths of murder ballad scholarship: this book sits atop the mountain range that is your work.

Thank you to the librarians, musicians, writers and scholars who assisted me along the rocky and confusing road to securing permissions for the song lyrics in this book.

Thank you to Lisa Perrin for holding a light at the end of the illustrated-creative-nonfiction-book tunnel, and for reporting back from the future to let me know it would all be worth it.

Thank you, my beloved Art Coven, for seeing me through this project with your encouragement, love and magic.

Thank you to my phenomenal friends, and everyone I spoke with that one day in August 2023 when I was so very worried that I could not do this. Collectively, you taped me back together so I could move forward.

Thank you, Sinéad Gleeson, for writing a total banger of a foreword. Your contribution to this book is an absolute gift.

Thank you to Frankie Armstrong for the lovely phone conversation that day in September 2023.

This book would still be an idea knocking around in my head without the brilliant women who made it a reality: Thank you to Alison Adler for seeing the potential; to my agent, Alyssa Jennette, for helping me add flesh to the skeleton that was the initial concept; and to my editor, Melissa Rhodes Zahorsky, for guiding me through this process, maintaining an unwavering trust in my vision, and making sense of the word salad that was my first draft (of anything ever).

And finally, I am enormously grateful to my family. To my mom and dad, thank you for supporting me on my path as an artist, always embracing the weird stuff I make. Daniel and Hazel, without y'all, I would probably get lost forever in the deep, dark woods of my brain. Thank you for being the earthly home I am so lucky to return to.

ABOUT THE AUTHOR

Katy Horan is an illustrator and interdisciplinary artist whose work has been exhibited throughout the United States and in Canada, published in several books, and four times selected for *New American Paintings*. Together with the writer Taisia Kitaiskaia, she co-created *Literary Witches: A Celebration of Magical Women Writers* and The Literary Witches Oracle Deck. She is also the illustrator of *Ask Baba Yaga: Poetic Remedies for Troubled Times*. Originally from Houston, Texas, Katy now lives and works in Austin.

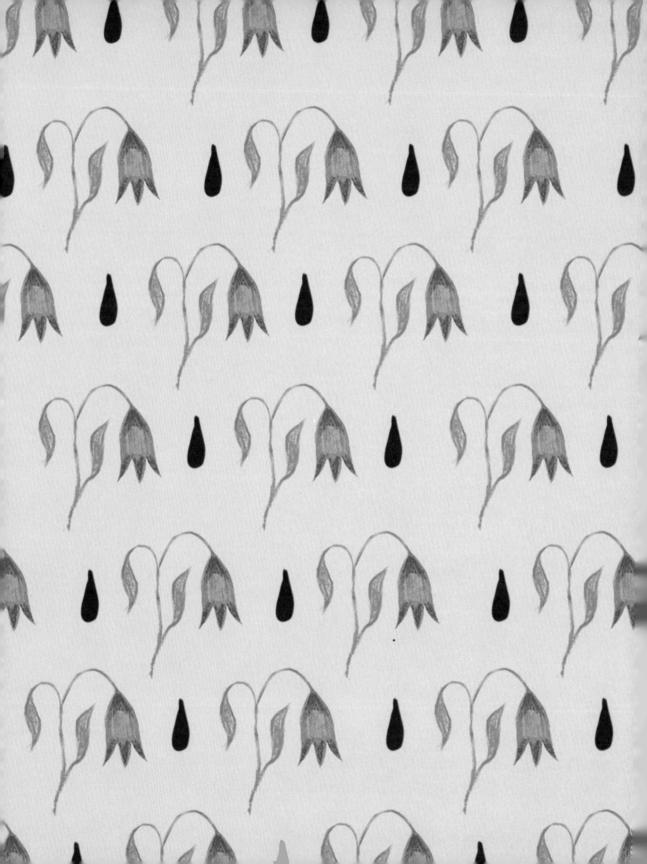